Another Use For...

101 Common Household Items

by Vicki Lansky

Illustrated by Martha Campbell

the book peddlers of deephaven, mn
Book Trade Distribution: Publishers Group West

Special thanks in putting together this collection goes to:
Julie Surma
Kathryn Ring
Jackie Leo, Susan Sherry and Susan Ungaro
at *FAMILY CIRCLE* Magazine

Cover and text design: MacLean and Tuminelly

Lansky, Vicki.
  Another use for-- 101 common household items / by Vicki Lansky ;
illustrated by Martha Campbell. --
  p. cm.
  ISBN 0-916773-30-2

  1. Home economics.   I. Title. II. Title: Another use for one
hundred and one common household items.

TX158   640.41
                                    QBI90-279

printed in the USA

introduction

Who among us isn't fascinated with creative uses for common items that we use every day? As a long time collector of tips and hints, I have been able to share so many favorites in my *HELP!* (Handling Everyday Life Problems) column that I write for FAMILY CIRCLE magazine. And now I have a chance to share one of the most popular parts of my column, which is called, *Another Use For...*

In addition to reading through these tips, feel free to write in the book to mark off those you want to come back to. Also consider photocopying those pages of special interest and putting them next to those items so you will be reminded about other ways they can help you (for example, the pages on fabric softener sheets might be attached to a wall or cabinet in your laundry area).

I have many more *Another Use For* tips than we had room for in this edition, as well as many more common items that would have taken us beyond the 101 we were limited to. But I don't have them all, by any means. If you have any unique use for an item that you'd like to share with me, please do (one idea per postcard). If I can use your tip in any future edition, you will receive a free copy of that book. Feel free to write to me.

Vicki Lansky
The Book Peddlers/Practical Parenting™
18326 Minnetonka Boulevard
Deephaven, MN 55391

PS. If you're interested in a free mail order catalog of my 20+ parenting tips books, just drop me a postcard at this address and we'll send you one.

CONTENTS

CONTENTS

Your A to Z Guide to Marvelous Multi-Uses for 101 Common Household Items!

- Keep a name/address sticker inside your eyeglass case. If you lose your glasses they can be returned to you.

- Get name/address stickers for your child and affix one to each item of school supplies—pencil, ruler, crayon box and such—and cover with clear tape. This will ensure against "loss" during the school day.

- Use a name/address sticker to identify yourself on coupons, to label books, records or other items you lend.

- Place one of your name/address stickers on each piece of wrapped Halloween candy you're giving out. The parents will then know that the treat has come from a concerned neighbor.

- Carry a few stickers with you to use when you need to leave your name and address with an item for repair or for another reason.

- Use rubbing alcohol on a cotton swab to remove the dust and dirt from the grooves in phonograph records without harming the plastic.

- Clean the tape head on the stereo-cassette player with a cotton swab or cloth dipped in rubbing alcohol.

- Clean paint brushes with alcohol, which will dissolve shellac and shellac-based primers.

- Remove grass and dye stains with alcohol instead of spot remover.

- Clean a sanded surface with an alcohol-dampened rag before staining or applying a finish.

- Use alcohol as a handy cleaner for the silicone caulking around bathroom tubs. It also shines chrome.

- Wipe candles with rubbing alcohol to clean them.

- To temporarily solve the problem of shoes being a bit tight, saturate a cotton ball with rubbing alcohol and rub it inside the shoes at the tight spot.

- Remove old wax from a floor before rewaxing by mopping with a solution of 3 parts water to 1 part rubbing alcohol.

- Dilute alcohol with water and apply it to plants with cotton balls to kill aphids. Or fill a pump spray bottle and use it to control mealy bugs on African violets.

- Dampen a soft cloth with alcohol and use it to remove hairspray build-up on a curling iron.

ALUMINUM FOIL

- Cover cookie sheets with foil. They can be wiped clean with wet paper towels, dried and reused for continuous cookie baking. And at the end of the baking session, cleanup is a snap.

- Wrap foil around doorknobs when painting, to avoid drips.

- Brighten outdoor lighting in your yard or at a campsite by placing shiny, reflecting aluminum foil behind the lamp.

- When rooting plants in water, place aluminum foil across the top of the glass and poke holes in it. Insert the cuttings. The foil will hold the cuttings securely in place and the water won't evaporate as quickly as it would uncovered.

- If you don't want your dog on the furniture, put pieces of foil on it. The rustle of the foil frightens the dog.

- Make a substitute funnel in a hurry by doubling aluminum foil and rolling it into a cone, reducing the small end to the required size.

- Use aluminum foil as a good, impromptu placemat.

- Wrap the ear pieces of your eye glasses with foil when your hair is being colored to prevent the dye from staining them during "waiting" time.

- If you use a color rinse on gray hair but like a light streak at the temples, wind up the strands you want lightened and wrap them in aluminum foil. Apply the color, according to the directions. When hair has processed, unwrap the foil-covered strands, and you'll have your natural light streak.

- Wrap heavy-duty foil around a panel of insulation board and tuck it behind radiators and baseboard heaters to reflect heat into the room.

- Place a piece of foil under the napkin in the serving basket and hot rolls will stay warm longer.

- Easily fix a small machine, such as a tape recorder or Walkman®, in which the batteries are loose because the spring won't hold them tightly: wedge a tiny piece of foil between the battery and spring.

- Polish the chrome on strollers, highchairs and playpens with a piece of wadded-up foil. This works especially well on older items that have begun to look dingy.

- Remove rust spots from car bumpers by rubbing with crumpled foil dipped in cola.

- Wrap kitchen matches in foil to keep them dry on fishing, camping and other outdoor trips.

- Put a piece of aluminum foil under the ironing board cover to reflect and make ironing go faster. Or, if you're afraid of scorching a fabric, place it between two pieces of foil and iron.

- Enjoy a cold drink outdoors by covering your glass tightly with a piece of aluminum foil and sticking a straw through it to keep insects out.

- Crumple aluminum foil into a ball to make a good pot scrubber, especially when camping, or to make a great cat toy.

- For winter protection, cover the vents on your air conditioner with aluminum foil.

- To save cleanup time on a paint job (oil or latex) that will take several days, wrap brushes in foil and pop them in the freezer. Defrost for about an hour before getting back to work. Also save cleanup time by lining your paint roller pan with aluminum foil. Keep "skin" from forming on the surface of the paint in the can by placing a circle of foil directly on the paint. Lastly, mix paints on a piece of foil for a disposable palette.

- When applying an iron-on patch, put a piece of aluminum foil under the hole in the garment so that the patch won't stick to the ironing board.

- To prevent staining a carpet when shampooing, place pieces of aluminum foil under the feet of furniture that cannot be moved.

- Keep cleaned silver tarnish-free by storing it with a piece of aluminum foil.

- Line the fireplace with foil, bringing it up the sides 4 or 5 inches. When ready to clean up after the fire is out, just fold up the foil and toss it in the trash. No mess.

- To stave off hunger in a hotel room when traveling, buy bread, cheese and aluminum foil. Make a cheese sandwich, wrap it in foil, then press it with a travel iron. In minutes you'll have a toasted, melted cheese sandwich.

- For craft/cover-up projects: aluminum foil can be spray painted.

- Line the burner pans on your stove top with foil and dispose of it when it's dirty. Also, spread foil on an electric oven floor (but not on the racks, because that will keep heat from circulating).

AMMONIA
- To keep dogs from getting into garbage cans, soak a rag or an old sock with full-strength ammonia and tie it to the handle of the lid.

- Get scorched spots off pot bottoms with ammonia.

- Wash away baked-on grease by first soaking the oven shelves overnight in ammonia. Pour the ammonia into a large, heavy-duty plastic bag, insert the shelves and seal the bag.

- Clean the oven itself just as easily, if it is neither self-cleaning nor automatic-cleaning. Warm the oven, turn it off, then set a small bowl of ammonia in the closed oven overnight. Wipe off oven walls and floor the next day.

- A good solution to clean combs, brushes and jewelry can be made with equal parts ammonia and water. On windows use 1/2 cup of ammonia per quart of water, plus 2 tablespoons white vinegar. For laundry use 1 cup of ammonia per load with half of the usual amount of detergent. On carpets and upholstery use 1 cup of ammonia per 1/2 gallon of warm water (clear ammonia only).

- Equal parts of ammonia and turpentine will take the paint spots out of clothing, no matter how long the paint has been dry. Saturate the spot several times then wash with warm soap suds.

- Clean golf balls by soaking them in 1 cup of water to which 1/4 cup of ammonia has been added.

- Put prepared gelatin in empty baby food jars and freeze. Pack frozen gelatin in your child's lunch box and when lunchtime arrives, the gelatin will be defrosted and ready to eat.

- Make a first drinking cup out of a baby food jar. Replace cap after you've cleaned and refilled the jar and punch a small hole in the top of it near the edge. Let baby drink away.

- Use clean jars as take-along containers for such snacks as Cheerios® or raisins.

- Pack clay inside the lid of a jar. Arrange dried flowers in the clay and screw the bottle, upside down, over the arrangement.

- Store nails or screws in baby food jars. Just nail the caps to a wood base and screw the jars into place.

- Buy garlic in bulk, peel the cloves and put them in baby food jars in the freezer. They keep indefinitely.

- Place a small candle in a baby food jar and put it in a brown bag to use as a luminary (it eliminates or minimizes the need for sand).

- Use baby food jar tops to make large-scale checker sets for kids. Paint them black and red and make a board out of construction paper. (They are easy to replace when lost!)

BABY FOOD JARS

BABY OIL

- Try baby oil to remove oil based paints from the skin.

- Rub baby oil gently into white rings and spots on wood. It may remove them.

- Blend a tablespoon of baby oil with 1/4 cup milk and add it to bath water to make skin feel soft and smooth.

- Use baby oil as a gentle make-up remover. Pat it on with your fingertips, leave for 10 minutes and remove with cotton balls.

- Rub lashes with baby oil to condition them, or for added shine instead of mascara.

- Add a little baby oil to wash water for baby rubber pants to keep them soft.

- Make bandage removal "ouchless" by rubbing baby oil around the bandage before you pull it off.

- Keep your stainless steel sink looking bright and shiny with a dab of baby oil. Dry with a paper towel, then add a few more drops and wipe again.

- To get rid of shower door scum and build up, apply baby oil on a moist cloth once a week.

- Remove stains from chrome trim on kitchen appliances and faucets with baby oil, applied with a soft cloth. Polish with another clean, soft cloth.

- Mix 1/4 cup of baby oil with a few drops of perfume or cologne for a scented bath oil.

- Warm a few tablespoons of baby oil and soak your brittle nails in it for 10 minutes to help make them more flexible.

- Rub baby powder into your pet's coat. Brush it out after a few minutes for a fresh, clean smell and a cleaner coat. Use it for a good dry shampoo for human beings, too. Rub it into hair, then brush it out thoroughly.

- Clean up hot, sweaty, sand-covered kids with baby powder. Sprinkle it on their skin to remove moisture, and the sand will fall off almost by itself.

- Use baby powder as an emergency face powder when traveling.

- Cover a stain on a white suit by rubbing baby powder into it, when you're on the go.

- When the powder that makes new rubber gloves slip on easily wears away, sprinkle in baby powder for the same effect.

- Prevent friction burns by dusting legs lightly with baby powder before you shave them with an electric razor.

- To untangle a thin chain, dust the knot with powder to make it easier to untangle.

- Sprinkle powder on men's white shirts both before and after ironing to keep the material from absorbing oil and grime during wear.

- To remove a musty odor from old books, sprinkle talcum powder through the pages. After several hours gently brush it out. Make sure the books are thoroughly dry before you try this.

- To cure a squeaky floor board, try dusting powder along the edges.

- On hot summer nights when sleeping is a sticky business, sprinkle talcum or baby powder between the sheets. It will absorb moisture, feels soft and smells good.

- Dust the insides of snoes with powder to help keep them dry and comfortable.

BABY WIPES

- Clean baby shoes with baby wipes.

- For a quick clean-up before company arrives, wipe down the bathroom surfaces with a baby wipe. Use a dry washcloth in your left hand to dry and buff as you move along.

- Blot a coffee spill on a rug with baby wipes. This will absorb the coffee without leaving a stain.

- Use wipes to clean dirty scrapes and bruises and sooth sunburn.

- Carry baby wipes in a plastic sandwich bag in your purse, and use them to clean up spills in the car.

- Let the toilet-training toddler use baby wipes for toilet paper. They're easier to use than toilet paper and will help save laundry. (Mom—use them on tender episiotomy sutures.)

- Keep baby wipes in the car to clean hands after pumping gas.

- To ripen peaches, avocados, pears, apples or tomatoes, put them in a brown paper bag. The paper helps retain the natural gases that ripen the fruit. Remember, as soon as you refrigerate the fruit or vegetables, the ripening process stops. Store mushrooms in a brown paper bag to keep them fresh.

- To keep onions on hand for two or three months without sprouting, remove them from their mesh or plastic sack and put them in a brown paper bag on the bottom shelf of the refrigerator.

- Tie a large brown paper bag over the head of your dust mop to shake off the dirt and dust inside the house.

- Drain fried foods or cool cookies on brown paper bags.

- Cut or tear a 10-inch strip along the back seam of a brown paper bag and slip it over your car steering wheel to keep the wheel cool and touchable during hot weather.

- Have a bag ready during the holiday season to save ribbons and bows as presents are being opened. Turn the top edges down about an inch and it will stand open.

- Remove wax from tablecloths or carpets by placing an opened

BAGS, BROWN PAPER

brown bag on the problem and moving a warm iron over the spot—quickly. Greasy spots will appear on the bag. Move clean paper area to the spot and continue until nothing appears.

- Kids find it satisfying to blow up old paper bags and smash them. They also like to make masks out of them. Just cut eyeholes and have them draw faces.

- Use a dampened bag as an emergency pressing cloth.

- Use paper bags to make big building blocks for forts, castles, towers and tunnels. Lay the bag flat on the floor or a low table. Fold the top over about 6 or 8 inches and crease the bag on the fold. Open the bag and fill it with scrunched up newspapers, putting in one sheet at a time. Fold the bag on the crease line and securely tape the bag closed.

- To save the trouble of scraping snow and ice off your car's windshield, place a ripped paper bag beneath the wipers when you park the car. Just peel it off in the morning.

- Line a kitchen wastebasket or trash can with an opened-up paper bag for easy disposal.

BAGS, MESH

- Peel several tomatoes simultaneously by putting them in a mesh bag and submerging them in a pot of boiling water for 30 seconds.

- Hang a mesh bag from the tub faucet or shower head to hold bathtub toys and allow them to dry easily.

- Hang a mesh bag from the inside of your locker at the health club to hold toiletries, making it easy to transport everything to the shower.

- Place a rolled-up mesh bag in the bottom of a vase to hold the flowers in place.

- Store bulbs in mesh bags hung in the garage or a dry basement so the air can circulate around them.

- For fast cleanups outside, hang a bar of soap in a mesh bag on the outside faucet. This way there is no need to remove the soap when washing hands.

- Take a mesh bag to the beach. When it's time to leave, bag all the toys and dunk them in the water to remove the sand.

- Make a suet ball. Pack suet into a mesh bag and hang it from a sturdy branch for the birds.

- Cut a mesh bag into strips and tie them together as you would a pom pom for a pot scrubber that won't scratch the surface of good cookware.

- Make a basketball hoop out of a mesh bag. Cut the ends off and thread a straightened hanger through the top, forming a circle. Hang it over a door, using the "hook" part of the hanger.

- Keep two or more balls of yarn or thread clean and untangled throughout a project. Place them in a mesh bag and thread the ends through holes on opposite sides of the bag.

BAGS, SELF- CLOSING

- Marinate meat in a self-closing bag. You use less liquid and there is no mess when you turn the meat.

- Use a self-closing bag to mix such ingredients as the stuffing for deviled eggs. When mixed, seal the bag, cut a corner off and use as a pastry tube to squeeze the stuffing out.

- Lighten your burden when you must go out to do your laundry. After separating your loads at home, measure the appropriate amount of detergent for each load into a self-closing bag and avoid having to carry a detergent box and measuring cup. Save the bags to use the next time you do laundry.

- Carry a self-closing bag in your purse to collect all of those gum and candy wrappers and the like. When the bag is full, empty it.

- To avoid staining your cookbook, put it in a large self-closing bag turned to the page of the recipe.

- Use self-closing bags for visible storage for puzzle pieces, name tags, seedlings or a lost tooth.

- Make a self-closing bag book. Simply sew several small bags together along the bottom edge opposite the closing. (A regular overcast stitch works fine.) Cut cardboard to fit inside the bags and slip magazine pictures or photos on either side of the cardboard. Change the pictures as often as you like.

- When you go to the pool, put your cordless phone in a self-closing bag to protect it from splashes. Carry your radio to the beach in a self-closing bag to protect it, too. At home, put your TV remote control in a self-closing bag.

• Organize and neatly store the various booklets and pamphlets that come with appliances. Punch holes in a self-closing bag to fit a three-ring binder, then slip each booklet into a separate bag and seal.

• Use self-closing bags to pack and separate small travel items such as cotton balls and swabs, safety pins, nail polish and the like. Or use large bags for various clothing items.

• Store small amounts of food in self-closing bags in the freezer, rather than in plastic containers, to save space.

Large Size
• Hang a large bag on the inside of a kitchen cabinet, broom closet or pantry door to collect aluminum cans for recycling.

• Protect hanging lamps and chandeliers from sanding dust and dripping paint when you work on the ceiling. Release the cover plate that is screwed into the ceiling and let it slide down the chain. Pull a dry cleaner's plastic bag up over the entire unit and tie it as high up on the chain as possible.

• Slip plastic trash bags between the mattress and box spring, and you'll find turning the mattress easier.

• Cut slits for head and arms in a big plastic bag and keep it in your glove compartment for use as an emergency raincoat.

BAGS, PLASTIC

15

- Punch drainage holes in the bottom of a large plastic trash bag that has an attached handle and hang it on the shower nozzle to hold bath toys.

- When it's time to take down the Christmas tree, place a large plastic bag (the type used outside for gardening chores) over the top and pull down to the trunk. Lift the tree from stand and carry it outdoors with minimum loss of needles.

- Need to waterproof a mattress? If no rubber sheet is available, simply split a large garbage bag and place it under the sheet.

- Keep a plastic garbage bag on a hanger in each closet. As clothes are outgrown or no longer worn, place them in the bag. When the time comes for a garage sale or a donation to charity, the sorting will already be done.

- Make an instant Hawaiian "grass" skirt by cutting narrow strips to within a few inches of one long side of a green garbage bag.

- When leaving for vacation, group your well-watered plants on a tray of wet gravel and cover with a large, transparent plastic bag. Put the plants in a cool place out of bright or direct sunlight. Or line the bathtub with plastic bags and cover them with a wet beach towel. Set plants on the towel and water them one last time.

• Slide a large plastic grocery bag over one end of a cat litter box, hold it by the handles and tip up the opposite end, spilling the litter into the bag. Or use one to line the litter box (less expensive than the liners sold for the same purpose).

• Use plastic bags to make dust covers for clothes. Cut a small hole in the center of the bottom of the bag and slip it over the top of the hanger for dust free blouses, dresses and sweaters.

Medium Size

• Before filling your humidifier, insert a trash bag in the reservoir, fold the bag over the top rim (snip if necessary for the float), and you have a throw-away liner.

• Store extra plastic trash bags right in the bottom of your wastebasket or garbage pail. You won't have to search for a new one when you remove the filled-up bag.

• Fold a plastic bag until it is the size of a package of gum. Secure it with a rubber band and drop into the bottom of your purse. You'll be surprised how often it comes in handy!

• Place dampened clothes in a plastic bag in the refrigerator if you plan to iron them within 48 hours. If it'll be longer than that, place the bag in the freezer. This is especially convenient for napkins and placemats, since you can pull them out and iron them as needed. Wrap colored and white clothes separately.

• If your car isn't garaged overnight in cold weather, cover your side mirror with a plastic bag, held in place with a clothespin, and it will be clear in the morning.

- Attach a plastic bag under the ironing board to hold pressing cloths, needle and thread for quick repairs, and a small scissors for snipping loose threads.

- Put an item to be spray painted into a plastic shopping bag which is much larger than the item, then spray it. No mess, no cleanup.

- For a quick, no-mess toilet cleanup, put your hand in a plastic bag while you scrub with a cloth or sponge. When through, remove bag and discard it.

- After a large dinner gathering, line a large mixing bowl with a bag and scrape off plates into the bowl for quick and easy garbage disposal.

- After the salad greens are washed and cut up, put them in a plastic bag and refrigerate. At serving time add dressing, close the bag tightly and shake well. (This is a good way to carry a salad to a picnic.)

Small Size
- Store bags of flour and sugar in plastic bags to cut down mess on cupboard shelves.

- Ice cubes stored in plastic bags will not stick together.

- Cover your shoes with bags and secure around ankles when working in a muddy garden or road.

- Use plastic bags over shoes inside boots to keep both shoes and feet dry in case the boots are not totally waterproof.

• Mix and knead the ingredients of meatloaf, meatballs or bread dough in a plastic bag. If your young cook doesn't like getting his hands sticky, let him wear plastic bags to knead doughs, mix meatloaves or grease pans.

• Keep a fragile item safe in a suitcase by packing it in an inflated plastic bag (blow up the bag, as you would a balloon) closed tightly with a rubber band.

• Set the legs of chairs and other furniture pieces into sandwich bags when shampooing carpets to prevent rust marks on carpeting and to protect furniture from moisture.

• Freeze wet washcloths and store them in plastic bags in the freezer. They are handy for soothing teething pain, cuts, bruises or burns.

• Carry a wet washcloth in a plastic bag for traveling.

• Make a funnel for liquids by clipping one corner of a plastic bag.

• When you're painting, keep a couple of plastic sandwich bags handy to slip over your hands if the telephone rings or someone comes to the door. Also slip them over kitchen faucets to keep them paint free.

• To protect a flashlight in the rain, put it in a plastic bag and close the opening with a rubber band. You can turn it on or off without removing it and the light shines brightly through the plastic.

BAKING SODA

- Remove coffee and tea stains by scrubbing pots or cups with baking soda and a plastic scouring pad.

- Baking soda is a non-abrasive cleanser. Use it without worry on fine china, porcelain appliances (including the inside of your refrigerator), stainless steel, aluminum and cast iron.

- To rid your hands of food odors, rub them with a paste of baking soda and water.

- After a wet bed accident, blot as much of the wetness as you can, then spread baking soda over the area and let it soak up the excess moisture. Brush off when dry.

- To remove stains and discoloration from aluminum pots, add 1/3 cup baking soda, 2 to 3 tablespoons cream of tartar, lemon juice or vinegar to a quart of water, and boil this solution in the pot for 5 to 10 minutes.

- Keep your refrigerator smelling fresh by storing an open box of baking soda on a rear shelf. Works in the freezer, too.

- Sprinkle dry baking soda on the rug or carpet to deodorize, then wait an hour or more and vacuum. Especially good for absorbing and deodorizing pet wet spots.

- Use a paste of baking soda to clean away corrosion on car battery terminals without having to use a wire brush.

- Keep 1/2 inch of soda in the car ash tray to eliminate odors.

• Use a solution of water and baking soda solution to clean and deodorize inside and around the door of your microwave. Or put a few spoonfuls in a cup of water in the microwave, boil for 2 minutes, then wipe down the inside with a sponge.

• To benefit a septic system, flush a cup of baking soda down your toilet periodically. Or use to freshen an RV tank periodically.

• Keep drains open by pouring down half a box of baking soda, followed by a cup of vinegar. After bubbling action subsides, flush with hot water. (This is a good way to dispose of that old box you've used to keep the refrigerator and freezer sweet smelling.)

• Use baking soda as a good, non-chemical facial scrub. Or as a regular or emergency toothpaste. One teaspoon in a glass of water also makes a good mouthwash. Try it as an anti-perspirant, too, straight from the box.

• Sprinkle a little baking soda into a laundry bag to minimize odors from soiled clothing.

• Keep a box of baking soda handy in the kitchen to extinguish a small grease or electrical fire, but not for deep fat fryer fires.

• Dissolve 1/2 cup or more of baking soda in bath water to soothe skin irritations from sunburn, insect bites, poison ivy and itchy rashes such as chicken pox.

• To remove black scuff marks from floor, rub them with a paste of soda and water. (Use as little water as possible to ensure best results.)

21

- Apply baking soda to absorb oil or grease stains on fabric.

- Use a paste of baking soda as a cutting board deodorizer. Rub board well and rinse.

- Remove perspiration stains from clothing with a paste of baking soda and water. Let it absorb, launder as usual.

- Clean fiberglass showers and tubs with baking soda sprinkled on a sponge. Sponge clean and wipe dry.

- To give a wood deck a weathered look instantly, combine 1 or 2 cups baking soda with a gallon of water. Scrub the solution into the surface and rinse off with clear water.

- Mix a cup of baking soda with cat litter to absorb litter box odors.

- Soak sour smelling dishcloths and sponges in a water and baking soda solution to sweeten them up.

- Add 1/3 cup baking soda to a wash cycle as a bleach booster or to the rinse cycle for sweet, clean-smelling laundry.

BALLOONS

- To keep a baby's bonnet looking crisp after hand washing, leave it dripping wet and fit it over a blown-up balloon to dry.

- Keep several small, water filled balloons in the freezer. Wrapped in a paper towel they can be used to ease the pain of kids' scrapes, bumps and bruises.

- Make your child a "cluster of grapes" costume by tying 20 or more purple and green balloons to safety pins and attaching them to his or her clothing. Use different colored balloons for a "bag of jelly beans" costume.

- For a special gift, stuff a dozen or more balloons with mini-gifts before inflating them with helium. Try chocolate kisses, wrapped candies, wild shoelaces, refrigerator magnets, erasers, dollar bills, coupons for personal services or special love messages, rolled into tiny scrolls.

- Protect a bandage on a sore finger by pulling a small, uninflated balloon over it before washing dishes.

- Tie a helium-filled balloon to a button on a toddler's clothes to help keep him or her in sight in a crowd. Tie several balloons on the mailbox or a tree near the end of your driveway so guests will be able to locate your party without any trouble. When camping, tie several helium-filled balloons to the tent so kids can locate your campsite. To help your child locate your spot at the beach, colorful balloons can be tied to the beach umbrella.

- For a unique party invitation, blow up balloons and write the invitation on them with a marker. Then deflate them and mail to your guests.

- For colorful ice in a punch bowl, fill a clean balloon with tinted water or punch, place in a bowl and freeze. Peel off the balloon when the liquid is frozen and the ice ball is ready for the punch bowl.

- Use balloons as place cards for a birthday party by fastening them to the backs of chairs and writing names on them with a marker or nail polish.

- Blow up a balloon and plop it into the paint can to keep a "skin" from forming on the unused paint.

BASTING SYRINGE

- Water small terrariums or the Christmas tree with a basting syringe.

- Fill your bird's water dish with a baster, right through the bars of the cage.

- Fill a baster with hot water and squirt over the icy area in a freezer to help defrost it.

- Fill the small compartments in a molded ice cube tray with a baster and you won't have to wipe up spills.

- Toddlers love to play with basters in the tub. Show them how one empties and fills.

- When you drop an egg, use the baster to suck it up.

- Use a baster to transfer varnish or paint to a smaller container that is easier to work from. Then clear the baster by pumping mineral spirits or thinner through it a few times.

- Use a baster to fill your steam iron easily and with no spills.

- When you've filled the coffee maker beyond the mark you desire, use a baster to extract the excess.

- Use a baster to siphon water runoff from large pots that are too heavy to carry to the sink.

- When browning ground beef or other fat meat, use a baster to suck up the grease from the pan.

- Extinguish flames in luminaries or deep candle holders with a water-filled baster.

- Blow up beach balls and other inflatable toys by removing the bulb of a baster, inserting the small end into the toy and blowing into the large end.

- A plastic mesh berry basket makes a neat sink strainer for kitchen peelings, or a colander for draining a single serving of pasta or for rinsing the berries you bought in it.

- Make a handy "cage" for a ball of string or twine. Pound a nail into the wall at an angle. Hang the berry basket on it and put the ball of string inside, with the end hanging through a hole. Tack down the opposite end of the basket with another nail.

BERRY BASKETS

- Use a berry basket at sink-side to hold soaps and sponges. Or staple one to the pantry wall or inside a cabinet door to hold small packages of mixes, seasonings and cold drink mixes.

- Place small items such as tiny lids or bottle nipples in a berry basket in the dishwasher to keep them from falling through the shelves and melting.

- If water collects and melts away soap in your tub soap dish, make a new one by hooking a berry basket over two stick-on hooks above the shower line but within easy reach. Water will drain away instantly.

- Use separate baskets to store small makeup items such as eye shadow or lipsticks. Spray paint them to match your decor. For a pretty countertop organizer, weave ribbons through the holes.

- Turn baskets upside down to make cages for toy animals.

- Make great geometric stencils for kids by cutting apart the panels of a berry basket.

- For nice Christmas gifts, line baskets with plastic wrap and fill with homemade cookies or candy. Wrap in bright paper and top with a big bow.

- When packing gifts for mailing, protect the bows by covering them with berry baskets.

- Tie a handle onto a berry basket, decorate it and hang from a tree branch for a birdfeeder.

- Add a capful of chlorine bleach to dishwater to make glasses sparkle and everyday silverware shine.

- To remove stains from baby clothes, fill a large non-aluminum container with a mixture of a gallon of hot water, 1/2 cup dishwasher detergent and 1/4 cup bleach. Stir until detergent is dissolved, then add the clothes and soak them for 15 minutes. Rinse well, and wash thoroughly before using. Be sure you are cleaning bleach-safe fabrics, and protect your hands with rubber gloves.

- Remove stains and fold marks from old or antique linens with a mixture of equal parts of liquid chlorine bleach and milk. Dab on gently with a cotton ball.

- To clean washable wallpaper, wipe it down with water to which you've added a little bleach.

- To remove stains from counter tops or a butcher block soak a white dishcloth with bleach, laying it over the stain for 10-15 minutes before rinsing clean.

- For relief from poison ivy, try patting the rash with a weak solution of chlorine bleach and water.

- Pour a cup of bleach into a stained toilet bowl and let it sit anywhere from two hours to two days. Scrub and flush.

- To scrub off mildew in grout use a stiff brush and a solution of 1/4 cup bleach to 1 quart of water.

BOTTLES (PLASTIC)

(Whenever you re-use a bottle, make sure the old label is entirely peeled off and the bottle is labeled for its new use. An easy way to remove a label is to wrap a damp cloth around it and let it sit for an hour or longer.)

Plastic Handled Bottles

• Cut a hole in the side of an empty, clean bleach jug opposite the handle and you have: (1) a clothespin container that will hang on the line (if using outside punch a few holes in the bottom for drainage), (2) a bird feeder, (3) a paint bucket for small jobs or, (4) a carryall for toddler's small toys such as legos and crayons.

• Pour your next 5-pound bag of granulated sugar into a clean, dry, 1-gallon plastic milk container with handle. Sugar will stay dry and lump-free and will pour easily.

• Use a plastic jug to catch old cooking oil. When full, secure the cap and toss. (Do remember to recycle car oil, however!)

• Make a "pooper scooper" by cutting a bleach container in half. Use the handled half to hold and the other half to scoop.

• Store pet or outdoor bird seed in a clean, dry milk container so an open box or bag won't invite mice into your cabinets.

• Use plastic jugs as garden "hot caps" by cutting off bottoms and placing them over seedlings. Leave the caps on at night but remove during the day when the sun warms things up.

- Make a "megaphone" for the kids by cutting the bottom off a plastic jug and removing the cap.

- Cap an empty jug tightly and use as a buoy for sailing races or while fishing.

Detergent Bottles

- Store cooking oil in a clean, well-rinsed dish detergent bottle. The squirt top makes pouring easier and there's no dripping.

- Blow dust from crevices of deeply carved picture frames, figurines and other hard-to-clean items by pumping a clean, dry squeeze bottle like a small bellows. Try it as a bellows for barbecue grill coals, too.

- Use a squirt-top bottle as a baster: squeeze it to draw in the juice. Be sure the tip is on tight so it won't leak.

- Fill a bottle with pancake batter and squirt into a hot deep fryer to make a treat that's especially delicious dusted with powdered sugar. Or, amuse the children by squeezing out pancakes in fancy shapes.

- Use a squirt bottle to hold shampoo, eliminating spills and controlling the flow.

- Fill a squirt bottle with water to keep in the car for cleaning the windshield when your car runs out of wiper fluid and for rinsing your hands after you change a flat.

- In the summer, give kids a squeeze bottle full of water and let them have a water fight. In the winter, add a few drops of food coloring to each bottle and let them paint the snow.

Soda Pop Bottles
• Cut the top off far down on the bottle for a funnel. Cut it off near the top and use the tall container to hold celery, bread sticks, or other tall foods or non-foods and supplies.

• Use a large soda bottle as a boot tree.

• Make the kids a hot weather, backyard sprayer. Cut 3 slits on one side of a 2-liter soda bottle. Insert the garden hose into the bottle and tape the connection with duct or electrical tape.

• There's no need for a heating pad or hot water bottle. Just fill a 2-liter soda bottle with hot water and rest your cold toes on it.

Lemon, Lime Juice Dispensers
• Fruit-shaped citrus dispensers are ready-made tree ornaments. Thread a 6-inch piece of yarn or ribbon through the little loop on the lid, tie the ends and hang.

• Remove the inner plug from a plastic lemon or lime, wash it and fill it with white glue from a large, money-saving bottle of glue. Fill another with hand lotion for a handy dispenser at your desk or kitchen sink.

• Use a lemon or lime juice dispenser as a fish pole bobber when fishing. Twist the line around the threads on the bottle neck and screw the top back on tightly.

Miscellaneous Bottles

- Use clear plastic bottles of assorted sizes to hold buttons. You might even keep one for white shirt buttons with two holes, another for four-hole buttons, and others for various colors.

- Clear plastic prescription bottles make excellent storage containers for sewing machine thread bobbins.

- Empty, squeezable catsup bottles with the flip-top lids have many uses around the shop. For example, store paint thinner from a gallon jug in one, or wood glue. They are also ideal for watering new seedlings and house plants.

- Decorate a small bottle to "preserve" tears, and run for it each time a child cries. The game will soon ease the pain.

- Deodorant roll-dispenser bottles can be refilled with tempera paints for children's art work, with water to wet stamps and envelopes or with white glue for craft projects.

- Plastic film containers can hold your quarters for the laundry, parking meter or toll road. They also make handy travel containers for hand lotion, and good "eyes" for snowmen.

- Fill a plastic film container with half an extra large foam hair roller (hollow center) saturated with nail polish remover and use as a traveling container. Turn one fingernail at a time inside the sponge to lift off polish, and recap when done.

BUTTONS

- Sew a button to each end of a drawstring to keep it from pulling through its casing.

- Remove buttons before consigning old clothes to the ragbag. Keep your button collection in a glass jar, both to add to your sewing room decor and to help you locate a special button quickly.

- Sew buttons on the cuffs of children's gloves so they can button them onto their coats for safekeeping.

- Substitute buttons for lost markers in any board game.

- Instead of a bean bag, make a wonderfully clicking button bag.

- Keep track of pierced earrings by fastening them through the holes of small buttons.

- Glue a pair of pretty buttons on earring backs you can get from a jewelry supply store. Or glue one special button on a stickpin.

- Nail or glue a button to the bottom of an uneven table leg to stop it from wobbling.

CANDLES

- Light up your dark and empty fireplace in the summer with an assortment of candles in holders. In the winter, throw candle stubs into the fireplace with kindling to help get your fire going.

- After addressing a package with a felt-tip pen, rub a white candle over the writing to seal it from rain, sleet or snow.

- When the metal tips come off shoestrings, dip the ends in hot, melted candle wax, twist and allow to dry thoroughly to prevent fraying.

- A wide-based candle makes a great pincushion. When pins are waxed, they slip through material easily.

- For an unusual painting, have your child draw a simple design with a wax candle onto a sheet of white paper. (The drawing will be almost invisible.) Then have the child cover the entire sheet with a watercolor paint. When the paint dries, the original "invisible" drawing will show through.

- Rub candle wax on sticking drawers for easier opening, along the track of your fireplace screen to keep it sliding easily and on snow shovels to keep snow from sticking.

- Weight hollow, decorative figurines and make them less fragile by filling them with melted candle wax.

- Fill a hole in a foam cooler with melted candle wax.

- Use drops of melted wax from an old candle as a temporary adhesive to seal an envelope, for example.

- Brace a rresh candle in a too-large holder with a few drops of melted wax from an old one.

CANS

Coffee Cans

- Make an umbrella stand from four stacked 3-pound coffee cans, with one end left on only the bottom one. Tape them together and cover with decorative contact paper.

- Line a coffee can with a plastic bag and keep it near your sink to hold small scraps and peelings.

- Use an empty coffee can as a waterproof toilet paper dispenser when camping.

- Use a coffee can, lined with a plastic bag, as a toilet brush holder.

- Nail coffee cans to the wall to make bins for clips, pins or other small items.

- Hold melons off the ground by resting them on the bottoms of empty coffee cans, pushed into the soil. The cans collect heat, making the fruit ripen earlier, and they also keep pests away.

- Make a fertilizer or grass seed spreader by punching appropriately-sized holes in the bottom of a coffee can. Cover the can with its plastic lid and walk your yard, shaking as you go.

- Use a coffee can to start a charcoal fire quickly and easily. Punch a few holes in the sides of the can, remove both ends and set it in the grill. Fill it abut 3/4 full of charcoal, add starter fluid and light. When the coals are ready, remove the can with tongs and set it in a safe place.

- Make a pair of stilts from two cans by stringing rope through holes punched in their closed ends.

Other Cans

- Recipes for some round breads and cakes call for baking in various sizes of cans. Muffins, pot pies and fruit tarts fit nicely into tuna cans. Be sure to grease the sides of all cans thoroughly before adding the food.

- When camping, take along tuna cans to keep ants from foods. Fill 4 of them 3/4 full of water and set a table leg in each can.

- Make an egg poacher from a tuna can with both ends removed. Place the cans in a skillet of simmering water and crack the eggs into them; the whites won't spread.

- Bury a couple of open-top soup cans in the backyard for putting practice. Be sure to punch holes in the bottom of the cans so rainwater can drain out.

- To keep saved plastic bags neatly in a drawer, stuff them into an empty paper towel tube.

- Use long tubes at the folds of stored tablecloths to keep them from creasing. Roll table runners and cloth place mats around the tubes to keep them smooth.

- Cardboard tubes of any size make ideal storage reels for bits of string, ribbon and yarn. Wind up each piece on the tube and cut a slit in the tube to secure it.

CARD-BOARD TUBES

- Slit a long tube lengthwise and slip it across the bottom of a hanger to keep trousers from creasing when you hang them.

- Re-roll wrapping paper inside a cardboard tube once you've opened it.

- Fold up appliance or extension cords and tuck them inside tubes for neat storage.

- Save space in suitcases or dresser drawers by stuffing knee-hi socks or footies into a paper towel tube.

- Use tubes as fire starters. Stuff 5 or 6 with dry twigs and leaves and stack them as a base. Add kindling and logs—and one match will light your fire.

- Store scarves wrinkle-free by rolling them around cardboard tubes.

- Save both long and short tubes to store cylindrical items such as knives or combs.

- Cut a tube into strips and insert them between stove top and counter to catch crumbs. Replace frequently.

- Fill short tubes with candy and toys. Wrap small things in colored tissue and close the ends with yarn for a pretty party favor for children.

- Cardboard tubes make acceptable hair rollers for large, soft curls. Cut the tubes into convenient lengths and fasten them with long bobby pins.

• Cover short tubes with contact paper and glue Velcro® pieces on the sides. Then let children use them for making free-form constructions.

• Wrap two-sided tape around a short tube. Insert two fingers into the end of the tube and run it over clothing to remove lint and dust from clothes or furniture.

• Make an instant boot tree by taping together 2 or 3 long cardboard tubes and standing them in the legs of your boots.

• Send kids' papers to and from school rolled in paper towel tubes.

• Help children operate light switches independently: cut a rectangular hole a few inches from the end of a long cardboard tube. The child can hook this over the switch and turn lights off or on by moving the tube up and down.

• Cut cardboard tubes into short lengths and use as rings around seedlings that are susceptible to cutworm attacks.

CARPET SCRAPS

- When working on any hard-surfaced floor, use two pieces of carpet to save your knees. Put them together with soft sides out—one to kneel on, the other to slide easily on the floor.

- Place 12-inch round carpet scraps under plants on the floor to catch over-watering excess.

- Use the soft side of a carpet sample to dust floors under appliances.

- Clean screens by brushing them with carpet scraps nailed to a wooden block.

- Cushion kitchen shelves that hold your pots and pans with carpet scraps to cut down noise when putting things away.

- To prevent black marks on vinyl floors caused by chairs being pulled in and out from a table, glue small circles of carpet remnants to the tips of the chair legs.

- Place a narrow piece of carpet on the floor between your washer and dryer. When something falls, pull out the strip and the article comes with it.

- Make a holiday doormat out of an edged carpet square. Use oil-based paints to write the appropriate greeting or seasonal design.

- Paint walls or other large surfaces with 6-inch squares of old carpet. You'll not only use less paint, you'll get things done faster.

- If you risk hitting the garage wall when you open the car door, protect the paint by tacking up some carpet scraps on the wall.

- Keep good-sized carpet scraps in the trunk of the car to put on an icy road for tire traction.

- Help define individual spaces for a group of toddlers by giving each a carpet sample to sit on. There'll be less kicking and shoving.

- Muffle the noise of typewriters, sewing machines and other appliances by cutting pieces of carpet to fit under them.

- Cut a section of carpet to fit into a pet's bed. Staple other pieces to an upright board to make a scratching post for a cat.

CASSETTE TAPE

- Tape children's music practice sessions to provide incentive and a good means of evaluation.

- Tape highlights of each day's study assignments as you read your text material. At cram time, play them back while you are doing something else, such as tanning or riding in a car.

- For a long car trip check out a book on tape from the library to keep you amused and alert.

- Pack a tape player in your child's camp suitcase and send your letters on tape.

- Record family history by taping interviews between your children and other relatives. Duplicate the tapes for gifts.

- What better way to share the sound of the holidays with those who can't be with you than by sending taped "letters." Let the kids sing songs, describe their activities and tell about their latest report cards.

- Play a favorite record or tape to get things started each day in your house.

- Tape record the sound of a crying baby to play that same baby back to sleep. Or tape the "white noise" of a washing machine or vacuum cleaner for the same purpose.

- During a thunderstorm, muffle the noise for a fearful child by playing a favorite record or tape.

- When you're too busy to play, reassure your infant by putting on a tape of your voices during a previous playtime.

- Dictate instructions on a tape and play them back as needed, while you knit or crochet.

CHALK

- Hide hairline cracks in plaster walls until you're ready to paint by rubbing ordinary chalk in a matching color across them.

- Drive a piece of chalk into a hole in a plaster wall and cut or snap it off even with the wall.

- Mark ring-around-the-collar stains heavily with chalk. The chalk will absorb the oils that hold dirt in.

- To reduce dampness in closets, tie a dozen pieces of chalk together and hang them up. Put a few pieces in a toolbox to absorb moisture and keep tools rust-free.

- Rub chalk on the blade of a screwdriver to keep it from slipping.

- Use leftover chalk ends to shine metal items from stainless steel cutlery to brass doorknobs.

- When the right and wrong sides of the fabric you're using for crafts or sewing look almost the same, mark the back of the material with chalk before you cut it.

- With chalk, outline your tools on the wall where they hang in the workroom. After you've used them, you'll know immediately where they go.

CLOTHES-PINS

- Use a clip clothespin to hold a growing plant to a trellis.

- When a tulip or daffodil doesn't blossom in the spring, push a clothespin into the soil at the spot. In the fall, you'll know where to plant bulbs to avoid gaps.

- To hold your plastic leaf bag open, shake it to spread it wide, then clip one side to the chain-link fence with two clothespins.

- To identify plants, clip to their pots papers identifying name of the plant, number of seeds and date planted.

- Clip a milk carton shut with a clothespin to keep milk from absorbing odors in the refrigerator. Keep paper and plastic bags containing chips or frozen foods closed with clips, too.

- Clip a recipe card to one of your hanging spoons or a cupboard drawer to keep it clean and at eye level.

- Use a clip clothespin to hold several tea bags together when making a pot of tea.

- Put a basket of clothespins near the hamper and ask family members to clip one onto any item that's badly spotted or that needs special attention.

- When hanging curtains outside to dry, clip clothespins to the bottom corners to prevent wrinkling. Inside, clothespins will help you keep curtains away from window fans or air conditioners.

- To prevent curling of the hem of a jean skirt or pair of jeans, after washing clip clothespins to hems about 5 inches apart, holding fronts and backs together.

- Make bibs for children of all ages by clipping dishtowels around their necks.

- Prevent a retractable vacuum cleaner cord from snapping back into the machine by clipping a clothespin to the cord at the length you want.

- After washing wool gloves, insert a wooden clothespin into each finger.

- To get the last squeeze of toothpaste, roll the tube and clamp it with a clothespin.

- Clip playing cards together to help little hands hold them.

- When grocery shopping, clip a clothespin to the edge of the upper small basket. As you find an item you have a coupon for, clip the coupon with the clothespin to save time at the checkout counter.

- If you turn your car lights on during the day because of rain or darkness, clip a clothespin onto your ignition key to remind you to turn them off.

- Fasten outdoor Christmas lights with clothespins.

- Use a clip clothespin to hold objects securely when gluing them.

- Use filters in your percolator for clear coffee and easy cleanup.

- Bake small loaves of bread in a Corningware® or ceramic pan. First line them with double coffee filters for easy clean up. Use a vegetable non-stick spray on the pan and then on the filters before filling pan halfway with dough.

- Use filters to cover bowls or dishes when cooking in the microwave.

COFFEE FILTERS

43

- When preparing a dish that calls for several different chopped ingredients, place each chopped food in a coffee filter to avoid spills. Also good when weighing ingredients on a kitchen scale.

- Line a sieve with a filter when straining oil after deep-fat frying.

- If your attempt at opening a wine bottle has resulted in floating cork "crumbs," decant the wine through a filter.

- Use filters as separators between your good dishes.

- When reusing a lid that's hard to clean, protect it by putting a filter under it before screwing it on.

- Put a coffee filter into your cast-iron skillet when you store it to absorb moisture and prevent rusting.

- Coffee filters make great holders for tacos or other juicy or messy foods.

- Wipe windows and mirrors with lint-free coffee filters.

- Use coffee filters to make snowflakes. Fold in squares or triangles and dip corners into bowls of diluted food coloring. Let dry before opening.

- Repotting? Line the pot with a coffee filter to keep the soil from leaking out through the drainage holes.

- Use a filter to apply shoe polish. Throw it away when you're finished.

- To stabilize fabric when doing machine embroidery, place a filter on the wrong side of the material and stitch as usual. When the piece is completed, trim away excess paper.

- Poke the stick of a frozen treat through the center of two filters. The drips will fall inside the paper, not on your child.

- Fresh berries and grapes will keep longer in the refrigerator if you store them in a colander, in which cold air can circulate around the fruit.

- Help prevent stretching by washing and rinsing woolens in a colander in your basin.

- Reheat rice or pasta by putting the food in a colander and pouring boiling water over it. Drain and serve immediately.

- Keep a plastic colander in the bathroom for your child to play with in the tub. Afterwards, store bath toys in it to drain and dry.

- When children are helping in the kitchen, pop your colander over spattering grease to prevent burns.

- An old colander makes a fine beach or sandbox toy for kids.

COLANDER

CORKS

- When you need to drill several holes the same depth, cut a cork to fit on your drill bit just above the depth you need. The cork will prevent your drilling the hole too deep.

- On your next boating trip attach a cork to your keys. If you accidentally drop them in the water, they'll float.

- Draw a simple design or your initials on the smooth end of a cork, cut away the material outside the line with the tip of a sharp knife. Press the cork on an ink pad and leave your mark on notepads, fabric, clothing labels, etc.

- Stick pins, tacks and little nails in a cork.

- Dull metal objects begin to gleam when you rub them with cork. Works wonders on brass lamps, knife blades and kitchen cutlery. With knives, the cork acts as a handle so you avoid possible cuts by keeping your fingers away from the blades.

- When lid tops come off pots and cookware, twist a cork into the screw on the middle of the lid.

COTTON BALLS

- Place a cotton ball at the end of a drawer runner so the drawer can't close completely and catch a child's fingers.

- Pour a little vanilla on a cotton ball and place it in the refrigerator to eliminate odors.

- Attach a few cotton balls to a pair of white tights to make a Peter Cottontail costume.

- Cotton balls make great fake hair for children's brown-bag masks. Dip the balls in glue and stick them on the bag for hair or a beard.

- Soak cotton balls with bleach and put them in discolored or mildewed corners of tiled bathroom areas. Let sit for a few hours before removing and rinsing the areas.

- Stuff a cotton ball into each finger of a rubber glove to keep long, sharp fingernails from piercing the rubber tips.

DENTAL FLOSS

- Truss poultry for cooking with dental floss.

- Sew buttons on heavy coats or other garments with dental floss.

- Use dental floss to repair mesh playpens.

- Hang pictures or sun catchers with dental floss.

- Restring necklaces on dental floss, and let the kids use it for bead-stringing projects.

- Slide a strand of dental floss under fresh baked cookies that stick to the cookie sheet.

- Use dental floss to repair umbrellas or leather stitching.

- If you must cut a hot cake, use floss. It won't damage the cake as much as a knife would. Floss even works as a cheese cutter.

- Use dental floss in place of twist-ties when closing a cooking bag to be used in the microwave oven.

DISH DRAINER

- In a child's room a dish drainer can hold books and records neatly upright. The silverware section can hold crayons, pencils or rulers.

- Organize and store plastic lids of all sizes in a dish drainer. They are easily separated and accessible.

- Use a dish drainer to store paper bags, shopping bags or magazines.

EGG CARTON

- Put egg cartons in boots to keep the tops from flopping over onto the closet floor.

- Cut the lid off an egg carton and place the cups in a kitchen drawer. Use them to store nails, paper clips, thumbtacks and other small items. In dresser or desk drawers or the sewing cabinet, they're great for storage, too.

- Use a styrofoam egg carton to pack small fruits for a picnic basket.

- Freeze extra meatballs in a washed styrofoam egg carton for another meal.

- Make ice cubes in clean, styrofoam egg cartons.

- Let your young artist use a styrofoam egg carton for a paint box. At cleanup time, toss the carton, mess and all.

- Make tiny bird feeders out of the individual cups cut from egg cartons. Tack them to porch posts or on window frames, then fill with suet or seeds.

- Line an egg carton with plastic wrap and use to store hard-boiled or deviled eggs.

- For a fireplace log starter stuff the cups of a paper egg carton with lint from the dryer. Melt paraffin or an old candle, pour the wax over the lint and let it dry. Cut into sections and lay under logs for a fire starter that will light immediately and burn for 20 minutes, long enough to start the logs. Or, to light the outdoor grill, place charcoal briquettes in a paper egg carton, one per section. By the time the carton is burned up, the charcoal should be lit.

- To make Easter baskets out of egg cartons, cut them in thirds and paint. Use a pipe cleaner as a handle. Add "grass" and top off your basket with a bow on the handle.

- Make a game for kids by removing the top of an egg carton and marking the insides of the cups with numbers "1," "2" and "3." Give each child the same number of pennies and let them toss away. High score wins. Or use for learning games of sorting.

- Place an opened egg carton in the bottom of a large grocery sack. When coffee grounds or other wet items are thrown away, the carton will absorb the liquid and you won't have a dripping trash bag.

- Store handmade Easter eggs, small Christmas ornaments or even golf balls in an egg carton. They also make cheap, light-weight and crush-resistant packaging for small breakables.

- Styrofoam egg carton sections make good bath tub toys.

- Upside down, they can hold tacos upright while filling them.

EMERY BOARDS

- Rough edges and small chips on the rims of crystal goblets can be smoothed by rubbing the edge *gently* with an emery board.

- Rub the soles of new shoes with an emery board to prevent slips and falls.

- When your sewing machine needle gets dull and you haven't another on hand, pull it across the fine side of an emery board several times at an angle to sharpen the point.

- File down rough edges of plastic utensils with an emery board.

- If the powder in your compact gets hard, rub an emery board gently across it. Use emery boards also to sharpen eye and lip coloring pencils.

- To raise the nap on suede, rub it gently with the less abrasive side of the emery board. Don't use a metal nail file; it can tear or damage suede.

- If pencil erasers become dirty or too smooth to do their job, rub them with the rougher side of an emery board.

- Use fabric softener sheets all around the house to eliminate musty odors and/or to provide a fresh, clean smell. Keep one in the refrigerator, especially if you'll be turning it off for a week or more. Lay a long sheet atop the clothes bar in your closet. Put sheets in wastebaskets and in packed-away luggage. Slip sheets into diaper bags, gym bags and laundry hampers, and put them in your shoes overnight.

- Remember that fabric softener sheets are designed to reduce or eliminate static cling—anywhere. Use them on venetian blinds and TV screens to keep dust from resettling. Rub a slightly dampened sheet on pantyhose. And another over fly-away hair and your hairbrush.

- Place a fabric softener sheet under the car seat to eliminate smoke odors, or just to give the car a fresh scent.

- Use fabric softener sheets to clean bathtub rings and to shine faucets and other chrome fixtures.

FABRIC SOFTENER SHEETS

- Clean a shower door with a used sheet. The soap residue dissolves away.

- Use a sheet as a filter in your dustbuster.

- Put a sheet in a pan with baked-on food and fill the pan with water. Let sit a few hours or overnight and it will sponge clean.

- Glue small pieces of fabric softener sheets to the bottom of knick-knacks to spare your furniture from scratches. Also glue small pieces to the back of pictures to protect the wall.

- Fit a used sheet across the floor register to act as an air filter, cutting down the dust.

- Run a threaded needle through a sheet to help keep the thread from tangling.

- Rub the areas on the back of drapes where cats sit with a sheet. It will not only collect hair but will refresh the drape.

- Keep pillows fresh by tumbling them in a clothes dryer for a half hour, along with several slightly damp, clean towels and a fabric softener sheet.

- Remove excess sanding dust from wooden items with a used sheet instead of a tack cloth.

- Stuff a few sheets in soft toys you make for toddlers. They keep the toys sweet smelling and self-softening, if you wash them.

- Place sheets between blankets being stored.

- Run your clean, hot iron over a used sheet to give it a smoother glide.

- Tuck a few sheets into your suitcase when traveling, to use with your hand-washables.

- Pin a sheet to the clothing of a child playing outdoors to keep mosquitoes away, or tie it in a belt or button loop.

- Use old sheets dampened with remover as tissues for removing fingernail polish.

- If you have a curly hairdo, use fabric softener sheets to roll your hair on. One sheet will make at least four spongy end papers.

- Save old fabric softener sheets, re-wet them with liquid fabric softener and use them again after they dry.

Liquid Fabric Softener

- Instead of scrubbing shower doors, apply full-strength liquid fabric softener to a clean, moistened cloth and wipe.

- To get hard water stains off windows, cover the stain with full-strength liquid softener. Let sit for about ten minutes before rinsing with a damp cloth.

- A capful of liquid fabric softener in a quart of water makes a great lint-free cleaner for glass and plexiglass tabletops.

- If you over-suds your washer, add liquid fabric softener to dissolve excess suds. Or spray suds in the sink after doing the dishes to get rid of suds without running lots of water.

- Soften new jeans or stiff fabric by soaking overnight (in your washing machine) in liquid fabric softener and water. Run through the rinse cycle and dry.

- To get rid of static on carpets during the fall and winter, spray with a solution of equal parts water and fabric softener.

- Rub your hands with fabric softener before stuffing pillows or children's toys with foam rubber chips. The chips won't stick to your hands and fly all over.

- Add a little liquid fabric softener to the final rinse of your paintbrushes to keep them soft and pliable.

- To help remove old wallpaper, fill a spray bottle with a solution of 2/3 hot water to 1/3 liquid fabric softener. Spray, wait 20 minutes and peel the paper off.

- Tint wallpaper paste slightly with food coloring so you can see exactly where you've applied it.

- To check for stopper-ball or stopper valve leaks in a toilet, put a few drops of food coloring into the tank and, without flushing, look for colored water coming into the bowl. If you see it, you can assume there is a leak.

- Distinguish hard-boiled eggs from raw ones in the refrigerator by cooking the hard-boiled ones in water to which food coloring has been added.

- Let children apply food coloring to cookies with water-color brushes, before or after baking.

- On Valentine's Day, add red food coloring to milk and pancake batter. On St. Patrick's day use green.

- Add a bit of food coloring to the bathtub water occasionally, to keep the kids interested.

FOOD COLORING

- Wear old cotton gloves or socks, dampened, to clean venetian blind slats.

- If rubber gloves irritate your hands, wear a pair of old cotton gloves underneath them.

GLOVES

- Wear an old cotton glove on one hand when bathing baby, to assure a better grip.

- For a great ice pack for kids, fill a transparent plastic glove with water and freeze. Enhance the fun by adding food color.

- Wear cotton gloves to clean crystal chandeliers. Dip your hands in an ammonia and water solution, squeeze out excess and wipe the prisms.

- Make a belt holder for small tools from an old glove. Cut two slits for the belt and cut off the tips of the fingers. If necessary, hand-stitch around the cuts to keep the glove from raveling.

- Worn out rubber gloves? Slice up the cuff for rubber bands; cut off the fingers and slip them onto mop or broom handles so they won't fall over when you lean them against the wall; slip two fingers over the jaws of pliers so they won't mar things; slip a single fingertip over your index finger when you need to sort through papers quickly.

- Wear gloves when putting on nylons to help avoid snags.

HAIR DRYER

- Keep a second hair dryer in the kitchen. On "cool," it can dry salad greens, on "warm" it sets the icing on cakes, on "hot" it defrosts a stack of chops or softens ice cream for easy scooping.

- If hard water spots your glasses dry them with a cloth, then blow dry to remove wet spots and lint.

- If you've left a freshly-baked cake for too long in a wax paper-lined pan, run your hair dryer over the bottom of the pan, then carefully invert it. The cake will drop out.

- To remove old contact paper from kitchen shelves use a hair dryer set on warm. Work on one section at a time and gently pull at the edges.

- Dry panty hose by hanging them on the shower rod and blowing them dry.

- Dry the inside of rubber gloves with a hair dryer.

- Quickly and safely remove candle wax by blowing warm air slightly above the drips. The heat softens the wax, which can then be wiped away with a paper towel, leaving no scratches.

- Speed up the defrosting process of your freezer by using your hair dryer. Never lay the dryer down inside the freezer, it's an electrical hazard.

- Defrost frozen pipes with a hair dryer.

- Use a hair dryer to quickly dry steam off a bathroom mirror.

- Use a hair dryer to blow dust from intricately carved wood work, delicate art work and artificial flowers—or even from behind a radiator.

- Remove crayon marks from wallpaper by using the hair dryer on it, set on "hot," until the wax heats up. The crayon will wipe off easily with a damp cloth and a small amount of oil soap cleanser.

• When a hot compress is needed, wet a hand towel in hot water and put it on the injury. Turn on the hair dryer to keep the compress hot; keep it moist with a spray bottle.

• Make bandage removal easy by blowing hot air on the tape for a few seconds to soften the adhesive.

• Clear up diaper rash by drying the baby's bottom with a hair dryer set at "warm" and held at least 6 inches from the skin.

• To remove a bumper sticker, use a hair dryer on it for a few minutes, then peel off.

• Use a hair dryer to blow powder into an itchy cast, or to dry stitches or sutures.

- If you find you've missed a few wrinkles in ironing a garment, lightly dampen the area with a washcloth, then blow dry with your hair dryer.

- To remove wrinkles from such plastic articles as tablecloths, shower curtains or shelf paper, use your hair dryer.

- Dry wet boots with a hair dryer.

- Use a hair dryer on the hot setting to shrink wrap a plastic bag around an object.

- When windows freeze shut, use a hair dryer to thaw them open.

- Loosen a too-tight screw by warming it with your hair dryer.

- Before you call the car-starting service on a cold morning, try blowing hot air from a hair dryer onto the carburetor. You can also thaw out a frozen car door lock with your hair dryer.

- Open windows in summer cause screens and sills to collect fuzz and pollen. For a quick cleanup, blow the debris back outside with your blow dryer.

- Blow dry your salt and pepper shakers after washing to keep the condiments from lumping.

- To release a snapshot stuck in a magnetic photo album, aim a blast of warm air underneath the page.

HAIR SPRAY

- Felt marker stains or purple ink from ditto machines on the hands can be removed by spraying the skin with hair spray, then wiping off. Try spraying lipstick and marker stains on fabric too, and even on gum. Works especially well on ink spot stains.

- To get rid of plant lice on African violets, use hair spray and a plastic bag big enough to hold the potted violet. Spray the hair spray into the plastic bag (never on the plant) then put the plant into the bag, twist or tie it shut, and let the plant stay in the bag for a day.

- Spray liberally on floral arrangements such as cattails, baby's breath and broomgrass to help preserve them.

- To keep the needles on your Christmas tree longer, spray as you would flower arrangements.

- Make an inexpensive gift wrap by spraying the Sunday comics with hair spray. It seals the ink and gives the paper a nice gloss. Kids love it.

- Spray the ribbons on outside wreaths with super-hold hair spray and let dry. Ribbons and bows will stay clean and wilt free.

- Use hair spray as a fixative for chalk drawings. Spray lightly and allow to dry.

- To stiffen ruffled curtains, spray them with hair spray.

- Spray recipe cards with hair spray to help keep them clean.

- If you trim your own or your child's hair over the bathroom sink, keep a can of inexpensive hair spray handy. Spray a tissue with it and while it's still sticky, pick up all those tiny hairs. Try the same trick on pet hair on upholstered furniture.

- To deal with static electricity, apply hair spray to the palm of your hand and, after each brush stroke, run your open palm over your hair.

- Squirt a bit of hair spray on your finger and apply it to the end of a thread. The thread will stiffen just enough to ease it into the needle.

- Spray a wasp or bee in the house with hair spray. It will stiffen the insect's wings, immobilizing it. Works on all winged insects.

- When you don't have enough barbecue skewers to go around, pass out straightened coat hangers.

HANGERS

- Bend both ends of a wire coat hanger up to hold sneakers or washable slippers after laundering. Use the hook to hang them on the line to dry.

- A simple way to organize spools of thread for quick selection is to untwist the neck of a wire coat hanger and slip the spools onto the straight part of the wire, then re-twist the neck closed.

- To make giant bubbles that will amaze your children, untwist the neck of a coat hanger, straighten the wire and recurve it into a large hoop with a handle. Pour bubble solution into a cookie sheet, dip the hanger loop in and pull it gently through the air.

- Make a paint holder from a coat hanger to keep your hands free when painting. Open the hanger and bend it in half, then bend it into an "S" hook over the ladder step to hold your paint can.

- To keep beads or belts from getting tangled, hang them from plastic coat hangers and hang in the closet.

- Straightened hangers, cut to convenient lengths, make ideal stakes for plants, indoors and out. Secure the stems to the wires with twist-ties, pipe cleaners or strips of nylon hose.

- Make a birdfeeder by inserting the wire ends of a coat hanger into the ends of the corn cob.

- Fashion a branding iron from an old coat hanger to scorch your brand on wooden parts of garden tools for easy identifications.

- Make a skimmer for leaves and debris on the surface of your small pool by straightening the hook of a wire coat hanger and bending the main portion of the hanger into a circle. Cut the legs off an old pair of pantyhose and attach the panty portion to the circle of wire. Sew up the open end with dental floss.

- If you've locked yourself out of your car, straighten a wire hanger, fashion a loop and work it between the window and the door. Use the loop to hook the door lock and pull it up.

- Punch a few more holes in an old hose and it becomes a lawn soaker.

- Slit hose sections and attach them with super glue to the edges of your play yard swing seats. The hose acts as a bumper if the swing accidentally hits one of the kids.

- Cover swing chains with a long section of garden hose for a steadier grip for little kids.

- Use sections of hose to insulate a lug wrench and a jack handle. This will give a better grip and your hands won't freeze when you use these tools in cold weather.

- Cut a length of hose and slit it to make ice skate blade covers.

- Protect a section of a young tree trunk with a piece of hose, slit and opened up.

- To store saw blades, slit a section of hose and insert the saw teeth into it.

- Run an extension cord through a slit hose when you need to protect it from traffic and weather if it will be laying across the driveway.

- Lay out the design for new, curved flower beds by using your garden hose to make the outline.

ICE CUBE TRAY

- Molded, plastic ice trays are good containers for earrings and other small jewelry. They also make good drawer dividers to hold baby socks and booties.

- Freeze pureed baby food in molded ice cube trays. Store the frozen cubes in a large plastic bag and defrost as needed.

- Freeze fruit juice in an ice cube tray for a baby or chill fruit punches without diluting them. For coffee drinks use cubes of frozen black coffee.

- Have fresh lemon juice all year long by freezing the juice in ice cube trays and storing in plastic bags.

- Metal trays with inserts can be used for baking. With inserts removed, they are an excellent size and shape for making molded cakes for which several small sections must be cut into shapes and fitted together.

- Use old trays to freeze hand creams and lotions that are then perfect for soothing anything from sunburn to chapped skin.

ICE CUBES

- Wrap an ice cube in a small piece of cloth and keep it handy when ironing to dampen wrinkles.

- Make scorches from an iron disappear by rubbing an ice cube over them.

- Remove candle wax on wood surfaces by first hardening the wax with an ice cube, then removing it gently with a table knife or spatula.

- To remove indentations in carpeting caused by furniture legs, place a single ice cube in the indentation. As it melts, the moisture will go into the fibers and plump them up.

- To remove gum, press ice cubes against it until it becomes brittle and breaks off.

- When coffee burns onto the bottom of the glass pot, fill it about 1/3 full of ice cubes and swirl them around vigorously. The cubes act like little scrubbers and will loosen and lift the baked-on coffee. Let the pot sit a few hours, swirling occasionally.

- To de-fat soup or stew, slide in 3 or 4 ice cubes. The fat will congeal around them as they melt. Remove the congealed fat, then reheat and if necessary, rethicken stew.

- If your hollandaise sauce starts to curdle, drop in an ice cube and continue stirring. The sauce will be smooth and creamy again.

- Combine all ingredients for an oil and vinegar dressing in a screw top jar, add an ice cube and shake. Discard what's left of the cube and your dressing will be extra smooth and well mixed.

- To water hanging plants and the Christmas tree without spilling water, put a few ice cubes into the stand and the pots and let them melt.

- To remove a splinter, hold an ice cube on it for a few minutes to numb the area for painless removal. Numb skin with a cube before plucking eyebrows, too.

- Use an ice cube as a quick pain-stopper for teething or a bitten tongue.

- Put a cube or two into a baby sock and tie the end. Let baby gnaw on it to ease teething pain.

- Before traveling with a cat or dog, fill a self-closing bag with ice cubes, close it tight and put it in a bowl. Cut a couple of small holes in the bag so that as the ice melts, the water will seep into the bowl for drinking.

- Let a puppy play with an ice cube on the floor.

- Smooth out caulking by rubbing an ice cube over it. The caulking won't stick to ice and the finish will be more even.

KITTY LITTER

- Make odor eaters for tennis shoes by filling the feet of knee high hose with kitty litter, tying the ends and placing in shoes overnight.

- To keep a garbage pail odorless after you've washed it with hot, soapy water, let it dry it thoroughly, then layer the bottom with 2 or 3 inches of litter.

- Put a bag of litter in your bathtub and slit it open when you leave your house for a long time. When you return, you should find no mildew.

- If transmission fluid leaks on the garage floor, kitty litter is a great, cheap absorbent. Pour a fairly heavy layer on the problem and let it stand for a day. When you're sure the absorbent action is finished, make a strong solution of detergent and hot water and scrub well, rinse.

- Sprinkle kitty litter generously around the tires of a car stuck in snow to give traction. Keep a bag in your trunk for such emergencies.

- Sprinkle kitty litter lightly on snow-covered driveways or walks to make them safe. (If you use too much, it will become soggy and claylike.)

- Kitty litter is a good covering for the bottom of rabbit, gerbil or hamster cages to keep them odor-free.

LAUNDRY BASKET

- Set a baby who can sit up in a plastic laundry basket to provide more stability during bathtime.

- Make cleaning up fun for kids. Use a laundry basket as a train engine, they can play choo-choo as they push it from room to room collecting toys.

- Top a laundry basket, round or rectangular, with a piece of plywood, 1/2 inch thick and large enough to extend a foot or so beyond the basket on all sides. Sand and paint the wood top and use it as a table for youngsters. When they finish playing, they can store games and toys in the basket.

- Invert one plastic laundry basket over another and tie the edges together, with your pet inside, for a handy transportation cage.

- Carry beach toys in a plastic laundry basket so you can easily rinse off all the sand from them by dunking the filled basket in water and draining it before you leave.

- Pack clothing, food and linens in laundry baskets when you're traveling to the cabin. Use one basket per room and/or person.

- When running errands, place a laundry basket in the car for all your packages. Small ones don't get lost and you can carry the full basket inside when you get home.

- Store your coiled garden hose in a round laundry basket.

LEMON JUICE

- Whiten discolored chopping boards with lemon juice. It will also work on yellowed ivory handles.

- Poached fish will be firmer and whiter if you add lemon juice to the cooking liquid.

- After cutting smelly garlic or onions on a wood board, rub the surface with a slice of freshly cut lemon, rinse well and dry.

- To get more juice from lemons, halve them, heat on high in the microwave for 30 to 45 seconds, then squeeze.

- Remove fruit or berry stains from your hands by rinsing with lemon juice.

- Stir a tablespoon of lemon juice into a cup of fresh, sweet milk when you need a substitute for sour cream or buttermilk.

- To avoid that funny aftertaste in diet desserts, add a squeeze of fresh lemon juice.

- Use lemon juice in the washer to remove rust and other mineral discolorations from cotton t-shirts and briefs.

- Use lemon juice to remove ink spots on cloth.

- Discolored socks will look white again if you boil them for a few minutes in a pan of water with a slice of lemon in it.

- Cut a lemon in half and use it, with a little salt sprinkled on it, to clean brass and copper items, and stainless steel kitchen sinks.

- To shine smooth aluminum, rub it with the cut side of a lemon.

- To eliminate odors in home humidifiers, pour 3 or 4 capfuls of bottled lemon juice in the water.

- Lemon juice is the natural way to whiten and brighten nails. Soak them in it for 5 to 10 minutes, then brush with a mixture of equal amounts of white vinegar and warm water. Rinse well.

- Write a message on a piece of paper with a cotton swab using lemon juice as invisible ink. After the "ink" is dry, hold the paper near a hot light bulb (not too close!). The writing will turn brown and you'll be able to read the message.

- The fastest way to dry up a facial blemish is to dab it with lemon juice a few times a day.

- When serving messy finger food like ribs or fried chicken, provide finger bowls. Float lemon slices in small glass dishes so that guests can rinse their fingers. (Be ready to enlighten anyone who assumes you're serving cold lemon soup.)

- Use lemon juice to bleach and soften grubby elbows: place a few drops of baby oil into two lemon halves. Stick elbows in the lemon, tape in place and leave on for 30 minutes.

- For blond highlights, rinse your hair with 1/4 cup lemon juice mixed with 3/4 cup water.

- End your dog's nuisance barking by squirting a little lemon juice in his mouth (not eyes) and saying "quiet" when he begins barking.

MAGNETS

- Keep a small magnet in your sewing box to pick up scattered pins.

- Use a magnet to tack a recipe card or any other paper to the refrigerator, the exhaust-fan hood, or the inside of a metal kitchen cabinet door.

- To retrieve hairpins or cutlery that have fallen in a drain, go fishing with a magnet attached to a length of stiff twine, or a section of a straightened coat hanger.

- Affix a few good-sized magnets to the inside of your metal bathroom cabinet. Safety pins, hair pins, tweezers, nail files and other small metal objects can be located quickly. Keep one in the kitchen junk drawer, too.

- Keep a magnetic strip on the wall in the bathroom to hold tweezers, scissors, and other small metal items.

- Attach plastic wrap to stainless steel bowls with small magnets to keep the wrap from blowing off at a picnic. Do the same with a tablecloth, if the table is metal.

- Use a magnet to collect steel wool particles so they don't get into the air you breathe.

- If you spill nails or screws, retrieve them with a magnet wrapped in a paper towel.

- Let a magnet help you avoid driving off without your gas cap. Attach a small one to the inside of the cover to your gas tank opening. The magnet will hold the cap while the tank is being filled, and the cover cannot be closed until the cap is removed from it.

- Keep a magnet in your tackle box to attract stray fish hooks.

- Use heavy-duty magnets to fasten holiday decorations or other items to a steel door.

MAYON-
NAISE

- To remove white rings and spots on wood furniture, wipe on mayonnaise, let stand for an hour and wipe off. For stubborn rings, rub gently with mayonnaise to which *fine* wood ashes have been added.

- Use as a soothing cream for skin that has been overexposed to sun, wind or cold.

- Apply mayonnaise to dry, brittle hair once a week as a conditioner. Leave on for 30 minutes, then shampoo out.

- Mayonnaise is good for removing tar. Spread a small amount into the tar, rub gently and wipe away.

MEAT
TRAYS
(STYROFOAM)

- The flat bottom of a meat tray makes a perfect stencil pattern. With an exacto knife or razor blade, cut out stencils for your children to color for Christmas cards or to decorate wood and fabric creations. Pin or clip the meat tray stencil to the material to be decorated and trace around the lines or fill in the spaces with paint.

- Use meat trays for disposable paint palettes for arts and crafts classes.

- Make simple puzzles for a toddler by pressing cookie cutters into the centers of meat trays and cutting around the outlines with a sharp knife.

- While you're busy sewing, let your child practice stitching on a styrofoam meat tray with a blunt tipped needle threaded with yarn.

- Use a meat tray as a pin cushion. The styrofoam sharpens your needles and pins.

- Styrofoam meat trays make good bath toys because they float.

- Be kind to your knees when working in the garden; use meat trays as knee pads. Use them as bleacher seat pads and boat seats, too.

- Cut meat trays into 1 inch strips for garden row markers.

- Meat trays can be used as cushions in uncomfortable shoes or as insulators in winter boots. Trace the shape of each foot on a tray, cut out and insert them into shoes or boots.

- Freeze water in milk cartons. Several good taps with a hammer to the four sides and bottom of the carton will produce great crushed ice for homemade ice cream.

- Fill a milk carton with whipped cream and freeze. When you need some, cut it off the top with a carving knife. Recap the carton with foil, secure with tape or a rubber band and return to the freezer.

MILK CARTON, WAXED

- For a quick and safe start for a charcoal fire, fill an empty waxed cardboard milk carton with briquettes. Light the carton and it will burn long enough to start your coals.

- When you have a lunch box to fill, cut a milk carton down to the size you need and use it to pack salads, desserts and such, folding the top down over the food. You can wash and reuse the containers.

- Use an empty, washed-out milk carton as a litter collector for your car.

- A spill-proof way to pour cupcake batter into muffin tins or pancake batter onto a griddle is to transfer it first to a clean milk carton. The carton's spout lets you pour with precision.

- When you're going camping, prepare casseroles ahead and freeze them in milk cartons, which fit well in the cooler and stay cold longer.

- Freeze fish by packing them loosely in clean milk cartons and filling the cartons with water. (When you defrost, save the water to use as fertilizer for your house plants.)

• Stash a couple of milk cartons and a few large stones in the car trunk to use as emergency flares if you are stuck on the road after dark. Put a stone or two in a carton to keep it from blowing away and light it—it will burn for about 15 minutes.

• A milk carton makes a good bird feeder. Cut out large windows on all four sides, leaving 2 inches at the top and bottom. Poke 2 holes through the top of the carton, run a string through and hang on a tree branch. Fill the bottom with bird food. Try decorating the feeder with adhesive-backed paper.

• A crushed carton under legs of heavy furniture helps it slide easily at housecleaning time.

• When you know you will be moving, start saving milk cartons for packing odd shaped dishes, vases, knick-knacks, jars, small sculptures, even silverware.

• Make a desk caddy by grouping two or four milk cartons together and drawing a slanted line down both sides. Cut the cartons along the lines and across the back and front. "Glue" cartons together by covering them and taping the rims with colorful self-adhesive paper.

MISTER BOTTLES

- Clean and shine chrome fixtures quickly with a mister filled with vinegar. Spray and wipe off.

- Spray the ironing board; it's a quick way to dampen clothes before ironing them.

- Keep a spray bottle filled with vinegar or bleach in your laundry room to use when needed.

- Save money on liquid fabric softener by diluting it with water and storing it in a mister.

- Keep a mister filled with water by your charcoal grill. When the fire gets too hot, or the flames too high, mist the coals with water.

- To prevent soot from spreading all over the house, dampen the ashes in the fireplace with a mister before shoveling them into a box lined with damp newspaper. Top with wet newspapers before moving outside.

- When you catch your pet in the act of misbehaving, squirt him or her with plain water from a plastic spray bottle—gentle and effective discipline.

- Lightly spray your face with water before applying makeup to eliminate the "made-up" look.

- A quick, easy way to clean a microwave oven is to dampen the walls with a mister, turn on high for 5 seconds and wipe down.

• Use muffin pans as stable containers for baked apples, stuffed peppers or even potatoes, in the oven.

• Pour gelatin dessert or pudding right into foil cups placed in a muffin tin for pre-measured servings and no cleanup.

• Freeze extra homemade broth in muffin tins. Measure the amount each cup holds so you'll know just how many "broth cubes" to take out as needed.

• To make ice cream cone cakes prepare a cake mix according to directions. Fill flat-bottomed cones 2/3 full, place them in a muffin pan and bake according to package directions. When cool, frost and decorate.

• Cook meatloaf in large muffin tins for faster baking.

• Muffin pans make excellent containers for children's fingerpaints or tempera.

• Use a muffin tin as a divider system in your kitchen desk drawer. Or in the workshop for small screws and nails.

• Freeze big ice cubes in muffin tins to use in party punches or large drink glasses. Add food coloring to the water, if you wish.

• Use small muffin tins to hold picnic condiments such as mustard, catsup, relish and onions on one "tray."

• Use a muffin pan as a tray for cold drinks to avoid worry that glasses will slide off a tray, especially if kids are the servers.

NAIL POLISH

Clear

- To keep metal belt buckles shiny, cover them with four coats of clear nail polish. Allow each coat to dry before applying the next.

- Use clear nail polish to repair small window shade tears.

- Before you wear new shoes, coat the areas that get scruffy with clear nail polish to keep them cleaner longer. Perfect for kids' ballet shoe toes!

- Seal a small hole in a plastic cooler made of plastic with a dab of clear nail polish.

- To keep a prescription label (or any other labels, such as those on cosmetics) clear and readable, paint it with clear nail polish. Also cover decals on children's toys that get a lot of wear.

- If you can't repair a loose button right away, try to keep it on by touching the center of the button, front and back, with clear polish.

- Use nail polish on a stamp or envelope flap that won't stick.

- When you've cut fabric that frays easily, immediately applying a thin coat of clear polish along seam edges will prevent it from unraveling when it is being sewn and laundered.

- Use clear polish to give a new gloss to old pearl buttons or to coat inexpensive costume jewelry that may peel.

- Repair a small hole in a window or auto windshield by filling it with clear nail polish. Put a few drops in the hole, let it dry, then put in a few more until the hole is filled.

- When making buttonholes by hand, mark the line on the material before you cut. Then, with clear polish, brush along the mark and let dry. This makes buttonholes with no loose threads or raveling.

- To keep ends of hair ribbons (or those on baby bonnets or other clothing) from fraying, dab them with a little clear polish. It seals the edges and lasts through machine washings. Use it also on the knots of small ribbons on lingerie to keep them from coming untied.

- Stop a run in nylons by painting the snag immediately with nail polish.

- Repair the little holes that develop in plastic or latex gloves with dabs of fingernail polish.

- If you want to cut down on your use of salt, seal up some of the salt shaker holes with clear polish.

- To prevent rust on the screws of a toilet seat, paint them with clear polish.

- Before setting shaving cream or shampoo in the shower or on the tub ledge, paint the bottom edges of the can with clear nail polish to keep it from rusting.

Colored

- For your child's protection, paint the tops of hot water faucets with red polish. It's easy to remove when you no longer feel the warning is necessary.

- For safety, paint the caps or lids of all containers holding poisons and also paint a big X on both sides of all these containers. Teach your child that anything with a red mark means "Stop, danger."

- For children not old enough to use the a phone properly, put a red dot in the 0 (for operator) so they will be able to ask for help, if it's ever necessary.

- Mark the bottoms of kids' favorite little cars with your initial in bright nail polish to identify them.

- Paint aging earrings with colored nail polish to give them new life.

- Put a drop of red polish on your golf, tennis or racquet balls so you'll have no trouble identifying them.

- Eliminate the problem of finding arrows or other markings on childproof caps on medication bottles by applying nail polish to arrows of both cap and bottle.

- If your measuring cups have lost their raised, colored gradations, go over the raised part lightly with colored nail polish to renew visibility.

- Mark the ounces on plastic baby bottles with red nail polish to save eyestrain.

- To thread a needle without hassle, dip the end of the thread in nail polish. Let dry and then thread.

- Before you insert the screw of a wobbly drawer knob, paint its point with fingernail polish. When the polish dries, it will hold the screw more tightly.

- Put a dab of red nail polish inside the waistbands of pantyhose with runs. At a glance you'll be able to see which should be saved for wearing under slacks.

- If you have poor eyesight, dab red fingernail polish at the temperature at which you normally set your thermostat, to make minor adjustments easier.

- To make adjusting water temperatures easy, after turning a shower knob to where you want it, mark the knob and the wall with a red dot so they can be aligned for future use.

- Dab red polish on the "off" button of your calculator, or camera flash attachment, as a reminder.

Nail Polish Bottles
- After painting, fill clean nail polish bottles with some of the

leftover paint and label them. Use for small touch-ups as needed. You'll find them much easier to store and use than large, nearly empty paint cans.

- Clean nail polish bottles make great non-spill containers for model paints since each color paint has its own brush attached to the cap.

NAIL POLISH REMOVER

- Use nail polish remover to erase the lettering on plastic margarine tub lids, so that when you store things in the container, you can note the contents on the lid.

- To remove burns on wood furniture, dip a cotton swab in nail polish remover and rub *very* carefully over the burned area. If the burn remains, scrape gently with a dull knife until discoloration disappears. Fill in with clear nail polish, one layer at a time, drying between layers. Cover with regular furniture polish.

- Remove scuff marks on floors with a piece of cotton soaked in nail polish remover.

- Use polish remover to remove bumper stickers. Gently scrape away with a razor blade or knife.

- Remove damaged lacquer coating on brass by rubbing it with nail polish remover. Then polish the brass or have it professionally relacquered.

- Use nail polish remover to remove paint on windows. Dab on, let sit for a few minutes, then rub off with a cloth.

- Use nail polish remover on a soft cloth or paper towel to remove scuffs from patent leather or white vinyl shoes. Rub lightly.

- To remove nail polish on washable fabric, scrub the stain with polish remover and wash as usual. Caution: never use remover on acetate fabrics.

- Use nail polish remover to remove ballpoint pen marks or paint from skin.

- To remove super glue from your hands, hold a remover-soaked cotton ball or cloth on the area until the glue disappears. Don't try to peel off the glue.

- Just a speck of nail polish remover will splice cassette tapes.

- Many watches have unbreakable plastic faces that can be easily scratched. Dip a cotton swab in nail polish remover and rub it over the face of the watch until the scratches disappear.

- Clean typewriter keys with an old toothbrush and nail polish remover.

- For a great non-stick shine on chrome fixtures, wipe them with nail polish remover.

- Clean your scissors with nail polish remover.

NEWS-PAPER

- Use newspaper to make a pattern for a costume.

- Use shredded newspaper to protect your packed breakables, as a mulch in your garden (wet down, so it won't blow away) or as emergency kitty litter.

- Pick green tomatoes when frost threatens. Wrap each one in 3 thicknesses of newspapers, and they will ripen slowly and beautifully. The newspaper absorbs moisture.

- Wet the straight side of a sheet of newspaper and place it on the glass next to wood you are painting, instead of tape. It holds easily, it keeps paint from windows and when dry, it peels off easily. If you're painting the outside of the house, fold newspapers over the tops of doors and close them. You won't paint the doors shut.

- If your outside door lets cold air in through the bottom crack, roll up a newspaper lengthwise and put rubber bands around it. (Cut it the same length as the width of the door.) Jam it under the door, or up against it, to shut out drafts.

- Dry newly washed windows with cheap, crumpled newspapers instead of expensive paper towels.

- Keep newspapers in your car. If your wheels spin on an icy road, several thicknesses of the paper under the rear wheels will give you traction.

- To get rid of cobwebs, make a disposable duster from a section of newspaper. Roll it tightly and secure it with a rubber band at midsection. Fringe one end with scissors.

- Make great newspaper logs for your fireplace. Roll stacks of paper tightly and push the rolls through tuna or small sliced pineapple cans. Wet down the rolls thoroughly (perhaps when you're watering the lawn), then let dry. Slide the cans off or cut cans off with tin snips.

- If a dustpan isn't handy, use a folded newspaper to catch dirt or dry spills.

- If shoes or boots are soaked from rain or snow, stuff them with newspapers. Lay them on their sides so air can circulate and dry them away from any heat source.

- To remove odors from a plastic container, crumple newspaper and put it in the container, secure the lid tightly and leave overnight.

- Protect your hands with big pieces of crumpled newspaper when you handle cactus plants. Cloth garden gloves don't work well because thorns in the fabric are difficult to remove.

- Use the newspaper comics section as emergency juvenile gift wrap.

- Use crumpled newspapers to remove oven cleaner residue.

NON-STICK VEGETABLE SPRAY

- Before using a spoon to stir something sticky or gooey, spray it with non-stick spray. Spray your spatula before frying, your beaters before mixing.

- Spray plastic wrap before placing it over a pie or cake and the sprayed portion won't stick to the frosting.

- Spaghetti sauce, or anything cooked with tomatoes, leaves red stains on plastic that can't be removed. Before pouring such foods into plastic containers, spray the insides well.

- Spray the surface of the table or counter before rolling out biscuit, pie or cookie dough. The dough won't stick and you can clean up with a few strokes of a spatula and a quick wipe with a soapy cloth.

- When making pizza, before putting dough to rise, spray the bowl. Non-stick spray adds fewer calories than oil and the dough is easier to handle.

- Spray connecting parts of the food processor before using, to make separating bowls and cover easier.

- Spray your broiler pan and the charcoal grill rack before using for easier cleanup.

- Spray sticking dishwasher runners; give tracks a quick spray to keep them from sticking.

- Spray cookie cutters to keep dough (real or play) from sticking.

- Having trouble making the coating stick on foods to be fried? Spray each piece before dipping in coating. This will also make salt stick to air popped popcorn.

- Use kitchen scissors to cut up raisins, dates and other dried fruit. To keep the fruit from sticking to scissors, spray with non-stick spray.

- Before using a grater, spray it. Such foods as lemon rind, cheese or onion will be much easier to remove from grater holes.

- Give the cap of your maple syrup bottle a spritz of non-stick spray before you recap it, to keep it from sticking.

- Stop squeaks in door hinges or oscillating fans with a quick spray.

- Squirt a sticking key with non-stick spray to make it turn more easily.

- To clean a dull shower door, use non-stick spray on a soft cloth or paper towel.

- Spray windows with non-stick spray before decorating them with artificial snow. They will wipe off easier when the holiday's over.

- Use non-stick spray on snow and garden shovels to help the snow or dirt slide off quickly and easily.

- Spray the bottom of your dog's feet, and snow won't pack between his pads.

- To dry fingernail polish, give nails a squirt of non-stick spray.

- To keep your pet bird's feathers from flying out of the cage and onto the floor and furniture, lay down newspaper sprayed lightly with non-stick spray when you clean the cage.

- Use non-stick spray on the hood and grill of your car. Bugs will wash off easily and the finish won't be damaged.

NYLON STOCKINGS

- Hand buff a wood floor to a beautiful shine with a pad made by inserting a folded bath towel into an old nylon stocking. The stocking will get snagged, so gather up plenty of old hose.

- Old nylons make perfect applicators for stains, varnish or polyurethane, especially in places a brush can't handle.

- Keep an old pair of pantyhose in your trunk to use to tie down the lid of your car trunk if you have something bulky to carry.

- Need an extra-large rubber band? Cut around the elastic top of an old pair of pantyhose. Two of these, crisscrossed, work fine when bundling newspapers or magazines. Use one to hold a bag in place in a garbage container, too.

- Make your own inexpensive softball that won't hurt kids or furniture: stuff an old sock with pantyhose and sew the top closed. Stuff dolls, pillows and toys, too, for softness and washability.

- Use old nylons as a "wick" to water houseplants.

- For great smelling sheets, put one nylon inside another and fill with 1/2 cup potpourri. Wet the nylons, tie in a knot and toss in the dryer with the sheets.

- To find a contact lens on the floor or carpet, cover your vacuum nozzle carefully with a piece of nylon hose to keep the lens from being drawn in. *Gently* move the nozzle over the floor.

- If it's difficult to scrub your back when bathing, center a bar of soap in an old nylon stocking and tie knots on both sides of it. Holding one end in each hand, seesaw it across your back.

- Carry some old nylons in your camping kit. In an emergency they can be tied together and used for rope. They also make good bags for children to put their collections in.

- A piece of nylon secured to a jar with a rubber band makes a good home for an insect collection.

- Slip the leg portions of stockings or pantyhose, with feet cut off, over an arm or leg cast. The nylon helps the cast slide into clothing easily.

- Store plant bulbs in the foot of a nylon stocking and hang them high to dry.

• When you've gathered pods from your garden for seeds, pull a nylon stocking over them and hang to dry. When dry, shake, and the seeds will fall to the toe of the stocking. Cut off, knot and store.

• Roll an old nylon into a ball and use it as a non-scratchy pad for cleaning sink and tub.

• If your skin is sensitive to a wool sweater, line the sleeves by tacking in the legs from old nylons.

• Old nylons make good ties for tomatoes and other plants because they're strong, yet won't damage vulnerable stalks.

• Strain lumpy paint through an old nylon stocking. Some interior painters strain *all* paint this way.

• Use a nylon stocking to hold mothballs in the closet.

• Use the waist elastic from old pantyhose to gather waists or wrists in children's clothes you sew.

• Stuff the toe of a nylon with catnip, knot and toss to the cat to keep her happy.

NYLON NETTING

• Use nylon net, folded into a pad, to brush up suede garments.

• Nylon net makes great interfacing. Use as many thicknesses as it takes to meet your requirements for stiffness. It holds up well through launderings.

- To get windows really clean, use nylon net to scrub them when washing. This works especially well if you live near salt water and have trouble with salt residue on the windows.

- To remove lint, put a yard of nylon netting into the dryer with wet clothes, using white net for light clothes, dark for dark clothes.

- Give an inexpensive, glossy picture the texture of an oil painting. Cut nylon net and wrap it carefully around the picture, taping the corners to keep the net flat and taut. Brush shellac on lightly, let it set for a couple of seconds, then carefully remove the net and let the picture dry. After it dries, the surface of the picture will have the texture of canvas.

- Instead of stones or broken bits of a clay pot, use several layers of nylon net in the bottom of flower pots and planters to provide drainage.

- To remove insects squashed on the hood of the car, use nylon net dampened in water to clean the car without scratching the finish. Try fastening nylon net across the grill of the car to make a "bug catcher."

- Use oven cleaner to clean the inside or bottom of an aging, crusted cast iron skillet or pot. Wash thoroughly afterwards.

- When all else fails, spray badly stained Pyrex or Corningware® dishes with oven cleaner. Put the pieces into a garbage bag, close it tightly with a twist tie closed and let it stand overnight.

OVEN CLEANER

Open the bag outdoors, keeping your face away from the opening (the fumes are dangerous). Rinse the cleaner off the dishes, and wash them thoroughly.

- To remove paint easily from metal objects such as lawn furniture or small objects like wooden picture frames, spray with oven cleaner, let sit for 10 to 15 minutes, then spray with highest pressure from the nozzle of a garden hose. Note: this will not work on baked-on enamel.

- To remove tough stains and rings on the bathtub, spray on oven cleaner. Let sit for several hours, rinse thoroughly.

- To clean a curling iron that's crusted with mousse, gel, or other hair products, wait until it's cool and spray with oven cleaner. Let sit, then wipe clean.

- Use oven cleaner for stains on driveways. Try 1 or 2 applications and let sit for a few minutes, then rinse.

OVEN MITTS

- Use oven mitts to grip a pineapple when cutting it.

- Keep a pair of oven mitts near the freezer to protect your hands when you hunt for items.

- Wear an oven mitt when you change a hot light bulb.

- Use an old oven mitt for dusting—one side for waxing and the other side for polishing.

- When ironing difficult things like puffed sleeves, put an oven mitt on and put your mitted hand into the sleeve. You'll be able to press into the gathering without flattening the sleeve or creating a crease.

- Put on oven mitts to clean a still-hot grill, wrapping it in several layers of wet newspaper. It will steam itself clean.

- Wear a pair of oven mitts when you wax and clean the car. In fact, keep a pair in your trunk for times you need to touch hot engine parts under the hood.

- Oven mitts make great gardening gloves for tough jobs like pruning.

PAINT-BRUSHES

- Keep a natural bristle paintbrush in the kitchen and at the grill for basting and brushing on sauces. The brush is more flexible and easier to clean than a regular pastry brush.

- Use a 1-1/2 inch paintbrush dipped in melted margarine or oil to grease muffin tins, cookie sheets and cake or bread pans. It's much faster than using a too-skimpy pastry brush.

- Keep a clean, old paintbrush near the washing machine for dabbing (instead of pouring) detergent on stains and collar grime, avoiding wasteful spills.

- To remove sand from such items as beach chairs or blankets, use a paintbrush. It can also be used for quick car cleanups, so keep one in your trunk. Foam ones can dust front window crevices.

- Use a 1-1/2 inch sponge paintbrush (used for trim and windows) dipped in soothing calamine lotion to "paint" kids' itchy chicken pox rashes.

- Cover seeds you've just planted by brushing soil over them with just a few gentle swipes of a large, old paintbrush.

- Use a paintbrush to dust wicker furniture and baskets—the bristles penetrate all those crevices as no cloth can (consider spraying brush first with an anti-dust product). Use others to dust carved furniture, or knick-knacks, too, or such things as plant stands, window sills, louvered doors, sewing machines and typewriter keys. They're also great for dusting leaves of plants (especially African violets).

• Hold pleats in place with paper clips when ironing.

• If you lose the pull tab on a zipper, replace it with a small paper clip. Cover it by wrapping it with thread to match the color of your garment.

• Paper clips are ideal for keeping bra and slip straps together.

• To get the last squeeze of toothpaste, roll the tube and clamp it with a large paper clip.

• Open clips up and use for Christmas tree ornament holders, in an emergency.

• If you're using cellophane tape without a dispenser, stick a paper clip under the loose end. When you cut the tape, replace the clip to facilitate the next use of the tape.

• Attach a pretty piece of ribbon to a paper clip for a bookmark that doesn't fall out or get misplaced. Use clips to mark pages in a textbook or manuscript, too.

PAPER PLATES

• Make a simple embroidery kit by drawing on a paper plate. Punch holes along the design and let the children sew along the lines, using a blunt needle with yarn or embroidery floss.

• Need one post card or an index card for a recipe? Cut one from the center of a paper plate.

- Prevent dripping when painting a ceiling by pushing the paint brush through a paper plate and securing it with cellophane tape.

- When cooking foods in the microwave try using a paper plate to cover the dish. It will not go limp and fall into the food or blow off the dish like paper towels or waxed paper.

- When packing for moving, slip paper plates between each dish. When unpacking, don't throw them away! Use them for quick meals while getting settled into your new home.

- Use paper plates as flash cards for learning shapes, letters and numbers with children. Correct answers can be "tossed" like a frisbee which can make it more of a game!

PAPER TOWELS

- Pick up tiny slivers of broken glass or spilled and scattered birdseed easily with a dampened paper towel.

- After oiling your sewing machine, stitch several rows on paper towels to absorb any excess oil before you sew on fabric.

- Remove candle wax from a carpet by putting a couple of paper towels over the area and pressing with a warm iron. The wax will melt and the towels will absorb it. Repeat until wax is lifted off.

- To remove silk from a husked ear of corn, rub down with a damp paper towel.

- Store cast iron cooking pots in a dry place between paper towels, leaving the lids off to prevent mustiness, moisture and rusting.

- Whiten a porcelain sink by covering the bottom of it with paper towels saturated with household bleach. Let sit for half an hour, then rinse.

- Grasp the skin of a chicken with a paper towel to make the skinning process fast and easy.

- Strain broth through a paper towel to remove the fat from it.

- Place a damp paper towel under the dishes on a meal tray in the sickroom, to keep them from slipping. It will also provide a handy way for the sick one to clean hands after eating.

- When serving food to little ones, use paper towels as placemats. If there are spills, just wipe them up and replace the towel.

- If you spill water on a book, place paper towels between the wet pages to absorb the moisture and prevent wrinkling of the pages.

- Remove crayon marks from a chalkboard by placing a paper towel over them and pressing with a warm (not hot) iron. As the towel absorbs the crayon wax, move it to a clean spot and continue pressing. Wash the board with a little detergent and water to remove all final traces.

PETROLEUM JELLY

- Brush a little petroleum jelly on shaggy eyebrows regularly to keep them in line and train them to stay put. And spread a thin coat on your eyelash curler to avoid sticking and pulling lashes.

- Put a thin coating of jelly on the rim of your nail polish bottle; it will keep the top from sticking shut.

- Apply a bit of petroleum jelly to the skin around your nails before painting them, if your technique isn't the greatest. Off-target polish will wipe off easily.

- Remove eye makeup with petroleum jelly.

- To make perfume smell nice longer, dab a thin layer of petroleum jelly on the skin before applying perfume.

- When home-coloring your hair, rub petroleum jelly around your hairline before you start so the color won't dye the skin and will wash off easily.

- Add a little red food coloring to petroleum jelly for a quick lipstick, and blue, for eye shadow.

- Shine patent leather with petroleum jelly.

- Keep vacuum cleaner extension wands sliding apart easily by putting petroleum jelly on the ends of them. Your artificial tree will come apart more easily after the holidays if you dip the ends of the branches into petroleum jelly before inserting them.

- Get lipstick stains off linen napkins by applying a bit of petroleum jelly before washing.

- If moisture makes light bulbs in outdoor fixtures stick when you try to remove them, rub a light coat of petroleum jelly on the threads before you insert them.

- Apply petroleum jelly to the insides of candle holders so wax will be easy to remove.

- If refrigerator racks tend to stick, wipe on a light coat of petroleum jelly to make them glide easily.

- To remove white rings and spots on wood furniture, try covering them with petroleum jelly. Let stand overnight before wiping it off.

- Before painting around window panes, dip a cotton swab in petroleum jelly and run it around the edges of the glass. (Don't let it get on the wood to be painted, though!) Any paint smears will wipe off with a cloth. And if you don't remove door handles before painting, smear them with petroleum jelly.

- Coat a clean and dry car battery terminal with petroleum jelly to prevent corrosion.

- To guarantee squirrel and ant-proof bird feeders, coat access wires or poles with petroleum jelly.

- If the pads of your dog's feet become dry or cracked, rub a little petroleum jelly into them.

- If a child's nose bleeds frequently, dab a bit of petroleum jelly into each of his nostrils once or twice a day to soften incrustations and scabs.

- When storing any chromium-trimmed item, such as a baby carriage, coat the chrome parts with petroleum jelly to prevent rust.

- Keep shower curtains sliding easily by applying a coat of petroleum jelly to the rod, then wiping the excess off with a paper towel.

PHOTO-GRAPHS, PHOTO ALBUM

- Send a photo thank-you note to gift-givers you rarely see—a picture of yourself using or wearing the gift.

- Take photographs of household valuables, furniture and other items to keep in your safe deposit box. They are evidence for your insurance claims in case of fire or theft.

- In your own family album you may want to include precious snapshots that belong to other relatives, pictures they don't wish to part with, and for which the negatives are long gone. If you have a good camera, you can shoot extreme close-ups of the photos you want, and you'll have a set for yourself.

- Rather than send out the usual change of address cards when moving, have a picture taken at a favorite spot in your old neighborhood with a hand lettered sign of your new address. Have the photo enlarged to postcard size and printed in quantity to mail before you move.

- If you're a working mom, have someone take a picture of you at work. Let your child take it to the daycare center. The teacher can start a "Mommy Works" board and all the children can take pictures of their moms at work. The children can refer to the photos whenever they need reassuring.

- Cut out pictures of familiar objects from magazines and put them in a photo album for a child's first picture book.

- Instead of throwing away second-best photographs, give them to your children to start their own family albums.

- Use a photo album to hold and protect your favorite recipes.

- Use a pillowcase instead of a plastic dry cleaning bag to store clothes. (Plastic wrap often causes spots if left on a garment for a long time.) Cut a hole in the end of the pillowcase for the hanger to poke through.

- Store leather or suede purses in an old pillowcase.

- Give an old pillowcase new life by painting on a decoration or message with liquid acrylic paint you can find in a craft store. Mix paint with water in equal quantities and apply with sponge brushes.

- King size pillowcases are just the right size to cover the pad on a baby's changing table. Use a king size pillowcase as a sheet for an infant car bed, too. If it gets a little wet, turn it over and use the other side.

PILLOW-CASES

- For an easy, no-slip way to bathe a baby, buy an inexpensive, plastic baby bathtub and slip a regular pillowcase over the *whole* tub. It forms a perfect soft hammock to lay the baby in, and all of the used water drains through the pillowcase into the tub.

- Use old pillowcases to store children's games. Sew velcro strips inside both sides of the open end and close the case like a self-closing bag. Let the kids decorate the cases as a rainy-day project. Use cartoon character cases as children's laundry bags.

- Put delicate machine-washable items, including pantyhose, in a pillowcase and close it with a rubber band or sew on snaps or Velcro®.

- When you strip beds, store the linens from each in one of its own pillowcases for easy transportation to your own laundry area or to the laundromat.

- Get cobwebs off walls and ceiling without scratching paint by covering the broom you'll use with a pillowcase.

- If you don't have enough cloth napkins to go around at a dinner party or buffet, buy a pair of pillowcases (they come in so many colors and patterns it should be easy to complement your tablecloth). Cut out 12-inch squares on both sides of the cases (don't include the hemmed area) with pinking shears. No hemming necessary.

- Carry and store sleeping bags in pillowcases.

- Use a pizza cutter to trim crusts from bread and to cut such foods as french toast, pancakes and spaghetti for the children, as well as bar cookies, strips of dough for lattice-top pies and greens for salads.

- To cut onions finely, chop as usual, then run over them several times with a pizza cutter.

- Cut popsicles in half with a pizza cutter.

- Separate bacon slices smoothly by slipping a pizza cutter between them.

- A thin-bladed pizza cutter does a great job of loosening sticky or painted-shut sash windows. Because the blade rolls instead of being pulled like a knife, it doesn't cut into the wood.

- A pizza cutter doubles as a terrific tracing wheel to mark your pattern as you cut the fabric.

PLASTIC LIDS

- If you buy hamburger in bulk and shape it into patties for freezing, slip a plastic lid between patties so you can pry off what you need without defrosting the entire package.

- If you've lost the sink stopper, set a plastic lid over the drain, with its rim down.

- Cut a plastic lid in half and use the flat edge for scraping cold fat out of pans, leftovers off plates and batter out of bowls.

- Use a plastic lid as a handy cutting board for a little jobs like cutting up cheese or onions.

- Plastic lids of all sizes are handy to use under containers in the refrigerator to keep shelves clean. Protect cupboard shelves by putting them under jars of cooking oil or syrup, too.

- Save a partial can of motor oil by covering it with a 1-pound coffee can lid.

- Make fine stencils for letters, numbers and greeting card designs from plastic lids. Draw the design on the lid with a marking pen and cut out the shapes with a utility knife. Hold the stencil firmly over an object to be marked and paint over it.

- Make a simple embroidery hoop for a child. Take the plastic lid from a large, round margarine container and cut out the center, leaving the rim only. Then cut off the bottom of the container. Place the embroidery over the top of the margarine tub and snap on the lid.

- Close a plastic bag with a plastic lid instead of a twist tie. Slit an "X" in the lid with a knife, pull the top of the bag through it until the lid is tight against the contents of the bag.

- Use plastic lids as coasters for kids' drinks, as saucers under plants, as spoon rests, or as drip catchers under paint cans.

- If you are always misplacing your keys, make a tag you can't lose by punching a hole in one edge of a plastic lid and stringing it onto your key chain.

- Use plastic lids as drip catchers under furniture legs, when you're painting.

- To keep earrings from becoming tangled in a jewelry box, hang a large plastic mesh square on the wall and fasten the earrings through the holes.

- Use large sheets of plastic mesh on refrigerator shelves and vegetable bins to keep them from wearing and corroding. The open weave of the canvas allows ample circulation, and it is easy to clean and durable.

- Cut plastic mesh and fit into the silverware section of the dishwasher so small pieces (like bottle tops and nipples) won't slip through.

- Use a piece of plastic mesh as a sink liner. Water drains through it, but it protects against scratches from pots and pans.

- Cut a plastic mesh collar to fit around a plant so cats and kids can't dig in the soil.

PLASTIC MESH CANVAS

POTATO CHIP TUBE CAN

- Use a well-cleaned potato chip can to store a ball of yarn or string. Punch a hole in the plastic top and run the yarn through.

- Use potato chip cans to package fragile items or homemade cookies for shipping.

- Potato chip cans make good canisters for such things as bread crumbs, flours, sugar or pasta. Cover them with adhesive-backed paper so they look good, then paste on a label noting the contents.

- Store kids' paintbrushes, colored pencils or crayons in potato chip cans.

- Transport such picnic items as 5-ounce cups, apples or baby food jars in potato chip cans.

RUBBER BANDS

- When taking covered dishes to pot luck dinners, keep the covers on by stretching a wide rubber band from the handle on one side to the handle on the other.

- When wooden pants or skirt hangers come loose, wind heavy rubber bands around each of the four ends of the hanger to keep the garments in place.

- Open a stubborn soda bottle top by wrapping a rubber band around it a couple of times to give you a better grip.

106

- Attach a cloth to each cleaning product with a rubber band to save the time and trouble of hunting one up when you're ready to get to work.

- To renew the shape of an old broom, put a large rubber band around it, a few inches from the bottom.

- If you don't have a "rubber finger" for your paperwork, just twist a rubber band around your index finger.

- Use a rubber band as a button loop extender.

- To avoid eyestrain when measuring a hem with a yardstick, place a rubber band around the stick at the desired height to help you locate the right measurement at a glance as you go around the hemline.

- When you're replacing a screw in a too-big hole, wrap a piece of rubber band around the grooves at the top before screwing it in.

- When you're doing odd jobs around the house, slip nails under a heavy rubber band around the handle of your hammer. They'll be right there, when you need them.

- Stretch a large, wide rubber band vertically around your paint can so that it cuts across the open lid. Use the band to scrape the excess paint from the brush each time you dip, and the rim of the can will stay clean.

• Use a wide rubber band to hold down the two contact points under the telephone receiver so that a toddler playing telephone can't accidentally dial long distance.

• Putting a wide rubber band around each end of the remote control for the TV provides a cushion to protect tabletops and also makes it less easy for it to slip off a table and be damaged.

• Stretch a large, soft rubber band around the completed part of the book you're reading as a book mark. It won't hurt the book and it won't fall out should the book be dropped.

• To keep pushed-up sleeves from sliding down, slip a rubber band over your wrist, about 2 inches from the bottom of the sleeve. (Be sure it's not too tight.) Turn the bottom of the sleeve up, covering the rubber band, then turn up again to form a cuff. Push sleeves up to the desired length and they'll stay put.

SALT

• A mixture of equal amounts of salt and white vinegar will clean coffee and tea stains from china cups.

• To dissolve soap suds in the sink or washing machine, sprinkle salt on them.

• Soften new jeans by adding a half a cup of salt to the water in your automatic washer, along with your detergent.

• To preserve the brightness of silk flowers, put them in a large paper bag and pour in two cups of iodized salt. Close the end of the bag and shake. After a few minutes, remove the flowers and shake off the excess salt.

• Pour salt immediately on spilled grease, a broken egg or a spill in the oven to absorb the mess so you can easily wipe it up.

• Discourage grass from growing between bricks in a wall or on a patio by sprinkling salt in the crevices.

• Sprinkle salt down waste pipes to keep them from freezing in very cold weather or to thaw frozen pipes.

• Make playdough by mixing together 1/2 cup salt, 1 cup flour, 2 tablespoons vegetable oil and 1/2 cup water. Store in an airtight container or plastic bag.

SHAMPOO

• Use a mild shampoo if you run out of dishwashing soap. (Not in the dishwasher, though.)

• Dirty bathtub floor? Pour on a bit of shampoo and use your foot to "scrub" dirt away. Be sure to hold on; the tub will be slippery.

• Use oily-hair shampoo to clean collars (after all, the "dirt" is nothing but body oil and soil) instead of expensive laundry products.

• To remove grime and grease from your hands after working on your car, wash them with oily-hair shampoo. It's a great grease cutter and is gentle to the skin.

- Add shampoo to warm water to clean hair brushes and combs. The shampoo will cut hair oils and leave your brushes clean and sweet smelling.

- When traveling, save space by using shampoo as hand laundry detergent.

SHAVING CREAM

- Apply shaving cream to spots on rugs or carpeting, then sponge up.

- Use shaving cream as a finger paint. Children can paint on a kitchen table or vinyl tablecloth. A sprinkle of powdered tempera paint or a drop of food coloring adds color.

- Use shaving cream in a work area to clean up hands. Wipe clean with paper towels for a waterless clean up.

- Use shaving cream to get rid of stubborn latex paint spots on hands.

SHEETS

- Place an old fitted sheet on the bottom of the top bunk bed. If the sheet has no pattern, decorate it with felt markers so the child looking up from the bottom bunk has a more pleasant view.

- To take down a Christmas tree neatly, lay an old sheet around the base of the tree as you un-trim. Then wrap the sheet around the whole tree and use it as a giant "sling" to carry the tree out.

- An easy way to scoop up leaves in the fall is to spread an old sheet on the ground and rake the leaves right onto it. Gather up the four corners and haul the leaves to the compost heap.

- To keep the inside of your sleeping bag clean, make a liner from an old sheet. Fold a twin sheet in half and stitch across the bottom and halfway up the side.

- An old sheet is often just the thing for making a banner to attract attention to a garage sale. Lay the sheet flat on a pad of newspapers and paint your message directly onto the fabric.

- In addition to the old, reliable, last-minute ghost getup, you can also turn an old white sheet into an instant octopus costume.

- You don't have to be skilled at sewing to stitch together three sides of two new, attractive print or colored sheets to make a blanket cover that looks like a pricey comforter.

- When traveling with children, spread a large sheet over the backseat and floor. When you stop, shake the sheet out.

- A twin fitted sheet makes a perfect picnic tablecloth; it won't blow up at the corners. Novelty sheets for children turn lunch into an instant party—especially at birthday parties!

- Create a stuffed animal hammock with an old sheet. Fold it into a triangle, tack one point to the corner and the other two along each wall.

SHOULDER PADS

- Shoulder pads are great for general dusting, and especially venetian blinds, because they're contoured and fit your hand. And they wash and dry well, by machine.

- Use shoulder pads as toy stuffing. The toys are soft, smooth and best of all, washable.

- Wax the floor with shoulder pads strapped to your feet.

- Use shoulder pads as mitts when you have to change hot light bulbs.

- Shoulder pads can be used as a strategic diaper additive for a baby boy.

- Fill shoulder pads with herbs and dried flowers to create a padded sachet.

- To keep your toddler from sharp table corners, tape old shoulder pads onto the corners.

- Use shoulder pads as knee pads around the house or in the garden.

- Using cloth tape, secure foam shoulder pads to hand rests on walkers and crutches to keep hands from hurting.

- Slip old shower caps over the bottoms of hanging planters before watering them. Later, carefully remove the caps and the accumulation of dirt and drips.

- Wear a shower cap when you give yourself a hot oil hair conditioning treatment.

- Your hands won't get dirty if you use a shower cap for protection when polishing shoes.

- If you run short of food covers, try a shower cap. It will work especially well on a bowl of rising bread or a large melon.

- Wear a shower cap on your hair when you paint (especially when painting ceilings). Throw it away when you're done.

- Place a shower cap over your face to avoid makeup stains on clothes when pulling a tight top over your head.

SHOWER CAPS

- Hang handbags, scarves, belts and umbrellas on shower curtain hooks suspended from the clothes rod or hangers in the closet.

- Run a hook through the top hole of a broom handle to hang it up.

- Use a metal self-closing shower ring as a key ring.

SHOWER CURTAIN HOOKS

- If your washcloths have folded tags in the corners, slip the tags through hooks suspended from towel racks and save space.

- Attach a hook to the clothesline and hang wash-and-wear garments on a hanger from it.

- Hang your shower curtain cap from an extra hook at the end of the rod.

- Use snap-on plastic shower curtain hooks to hold toys and rattles on a baby's crib.

- Save closet space by slipping a hook over the necks of some hangers, then suspending other hangers from them.

SHOWER CURTAINS/ PLASTIC TABLE-CLOTHS

- Put a shower curtain or plastic tablecloth under a pattern you're cutting to make scissors glide across the surface more easily and to protect the tabletop.

- Use either a shower curtain or a tablecloth as a table protector for a plant display or to cover a table or counter when you're repotting plants indoors.

- Slip a protective plastic cloth or curtain between sheets and bedpad with a child who wets at night.

- Cover anything outdoors—including yourself—with a plastic cloth or curtain in a sudden rain.

- Use a plastic tablecloth or shower curtain as a picnic tablecloth.

- A vinyl tablecloth makes a great "magic carpet" for kids, especially if it's fringed.

- Cut shelf liners from old vinyl tablecloths. Flannel-backed ones adhere well.

- Protect your dining table from moisture from spills or sweating glasses by spreading a flannel-backed vinyl tablecloth under table pads or your linen cloth.

- Can't find a cover to fit the grill? Use a colorful old vinyl tablecloth, fastened to the grill with tablecloth grips.

- Hang an old shower curtain behind lightweight draperies in the winter to insulate the room against cold drafts.

- Make curtains for basement windows out of shower curtains.

- Protect carpeting in bad weather by using strips of a heavy plastic shower curtain or liner.

- Use a shower curtain liner as a drop cloth when painting. It's heavier and more durable than the cloths sold for that purpose.

- Protect a small, inflatable kiddie pool from damage from rocks and twigs by spreading a shower curtain liner beneath it.

- Make a full-length apron for messy jobs by cutting a cobbler pattern from a shower curtain and attaching ties at neck and waist. Or convert one into a make-up cape.

SOAP

- Tie old soap bits into an old nylon stocking. Let it dangle in the water for a moment before you swish to make suds.

- Let slivers of soap dry out and use them to trace out patterns on cloth. Or put them into a soap mitt made by sewing two washcloths together on three sides.

- Instead of using bubble bath, hold soap under a fast-running faucet to fill the tub with bubbles. (Ivory soap works especially well.)

- When insect bites cause discomfort, moisten a bar of soap and rub it on the affected area. When it dries, the skin will feel "anesthetized."

- Lubricate a cranky zipper by rubbing the teeth with a bar of soap.

- An unwrapped bar of soap will keep a drawer or linen closet smelling pleasant. Also put one in with your stored off-season clothes.

- Use the bathroom mirror for messages. A bar of soap is your "pencil."

- Use a covered bar of soap as a pin cushion. It makes sewing much easier as needles will just glide through the fabric. Keep a bar at the baby's changing table to stick diaper pins into, too.

- Hang bars of deodorant soap around crops to repulse deer.

- Rub sticking drawers and windows with soap to make them open more easily.

- To eliminate the need for scraping windows when finished painting, rub a bar of softened soap around the window panes, being sure not to soap the wood.

- Keep a bar of soap near the workbench to run a handsaw blade across before sawing wood. Nails and screws will also go in easier if rubbed with soap first.

- To fill small holes in a wall, rub a bar of soap over the wall until it looks flat and even, then paint.

- Make decorative snow at Christmas time from a thick solution of powdered soap flakes and water. Beat at high speed with electric mixer until stiff.

- Before you put pots and pans on an open fire, thinly coat their bottoms with a bar of soap. Cleaning the soot off afterward will be much easier.

- Apartment-dwelling families with active youngsters can keep those who live on the floor below them happy by having the kids wear big, heavy socks over their shoes.

- Put a sock over the broom handle and secure it with a rubber band, then no matter where you prop your broom the walls won't become scarred. Works with ladder legs, too.

SOCKS

- A tube sock slipped over a rolling pin keeps it free of dust.

- Protect floors when moving heavy furniture by slipping an old sock over each leg.

- Slip an old pair of socks over your hands when rubbing off metal polish. Silver or brass surfaces will glow radiantly.

- Insert a yardstick in an old tube sock and tie at the cuff to make a great duster for walls behind radiators and floors under low furniture and appliances.

- Saturate an old sock in bleach and throw it in with the other whites to be washed to avoid wasting bleach.

- If you're a fresh air clothesline buff, keep an old sock in the clothespin bag to clean dust from the line before hanging clothes.

- Cut off the top ribbing of a white sock and use it for an instant knee or elbow bandage cover. To cover an arm cast, cut the toe off a tube sock and pull it over the cast. Cut a place for the thumb.

- The tops of socks can be cut off and used as wrist sweat bands. Or even ponytail holders.

- Keep a toddler from opening a door by securing a sock to the doorknob with a rubber band.

- Place a cotton sock over a drinking glass or bottle to keep it from slipping out of small hands.

• Save old socks and use them to dust furniture. Simply slip over your "dusting" hand. Keep some in the car, too, to protect your hands if you have to change a tire.

• Make kneepads to protect a crawling baby's knees and keep pants from wearing out. Cut the toes off an old athletic sock and pull it on over baby's pants.

• Before putting on coats, use old socks as fingerless mittens for toddlers. The socks' length will help keep them on. For older kids, cut holes out for fingers in other socks to be worn under gloves to give additional warmth to hands and wrists.

• Make an inexpensive softball that won't hurt kids or furniture by stuffing an old sock with nylons and sewing shut. For a bean bag, fill the foot of a sock with beans and sew it up.

• Pack shoes in old socks when you travel.

- Keep kids' toes warm by covering their ice skates with large wool socks with slits cut in the bottom for the skate blades.

- Dress up a water bottle with a colored sock to absorb the moisture from the outside of the bottle while making a fashion statement, especially at your exercise class.

- Make hand puppets for your kids' own shows from old socks or mittens. Add yarn for hair and buttons for facial features.

- Put a dog's squeaky toy or a golf ball in an old sock, knot it and TOSS!

- Pack fragile knick-knacks (like ceramic Christmas decorations) in old socks. Unlike tissue, the wrapping doesn't tear or take up much space.

SPONGES

- A dampened sponge will remove lint from clothing or furniture.

- Keep a sponge at the base of the umbrella stand to soak up water.

- Sponges are ideal for texturing paint on walls or furniture. Just press the sponge into the wet paint and pull it straight up. Use sponges also for painting difficult things like wrought iron railings, wire fencing or carved furniture.

- Use cut up latex sponges as wedges for makeup.

- Put a sponge under a pot you're scouring to keep it from scratching the sink.

- Cut a sponge to fit a soap dish, and it will absorb water and film from the soap. You'll also have a handy sponge with which to clean the sink.

- To make your own fabric softener sheets, store quarters of a small sponge in a jar with a small amount of liquid fabric softener. On washday, squeeze the excess out of a piece of sponge and throw it in the dryer.

- If you must kneel to clean your bathtub, protect your knees with two sponges.

- Make a kitchen garden with sprouts and a sponge in a dish of water.

- To remove a broken lightbulb first unplug and turn off the lamp. Then, press a thick, dry sponge onto the jagged bulb base and twist gently.

- To pack or store an odd-shaped ceramic piece or bowl, wet a sponge and put the piece on it. Let it dry, and when the sponge dries, it will form the proper indentation to hold the piece safely in position.

- Wet and freeze small sponges to be used when an ice compress is needed.

- Cut a sponge into puzzle pieces for a child. Or buy a package of different colored sponges and cut them into shapes to use as "blocks" in or out of the bathtub.

SQUEEGEES
- Use a squeegee to clean the tiles and shower doors after a shower.

- Scrape cat fur off furniture with a squeegee.

- A small squeegee is good for scraping crumbs off the tablecloth.

- Eliminate bubbles and wrinkles in vinyl wall coverings by pulling a squeegee down it as you put it in place.

- Scrape loosened ice from the inside of your freezer with a squeegee.

STEEL WOOL
- To keep bits of steel wool from pricking your skin, pack it into an orange half, with pulp removed. You can press down hard on the orange without hurting your hand.

- Stuff a homemade pin cushion with steel wool. It will help keep the pins and needles sharp.

- When bathing cats or dogs, place steel wool in the drain opening to catch hairs and keep the drain from clogging.

- Wind a few strands of steel wool around the threads of a screw before you screw it in.

- Use steel wool to gently rub crayon marks from wallpaper.

- To keep strings on pull toys from getting tangled in the wheels, draw the string through a plastic straw, and knot it to the toy.

- To make croquet wickets more visible on the lawn, run them through colorful straws before putting them in the ground.

- To make a magic wand, just attach a star to a straw.

- Let kids string cut sections of straws for necklaces. They're likely to last longer than cereal or macaroni pieces.

- To use a straw as a bubble blower, cut the tip diagonally.

- If the pilot light in a gas range goes out, light one end of a paper drinking straw and use it instead of a match. The extra length makes lighting hurricane candles easier, too.

- Preserve food longer in a self-closing bag from which you've removed all air. Close the bag just far enough to allow a straw to be inserted in a corner. Suck air out through the straw, then remove it and seal the bag completely.

- Make portable condiment shakers by filling cut pieces of straw with salt and pepper and twisting the ends up.

- To speed up slow-moving ketchup, push a straw down into the bottle when it is first opened. It adds air which starts the flow.

- To mark a stitch in knitting, cut a 1/8 inch slice off a straw. This straw ring will fit on needles up to size 10.

STRAWS

• Keep fine chain jewelry from getting tangled by slipping it through a straw, then fastening the catch.

• Insert flower stems that are damaged or too short for your vase into plastic straws cut to the length you need.

TAPE, MASKING

• When taking something apart, lay out each tiny piece in order on a length of masking tape to keep them all safely until they are needed.

• Cover a plywood cut-line with masking tape before you saw it, to keep the wood from splitting.

• When doing household jobs, protect your fingernails by putting a strip of masking tape over each one before you slip on the gloves.

• Wrap masking tape around the metal on a paintbrush before dipping it in paint to make cleaning the brush easier.

• Reinforce the back of a piece of sandpaper with masking tape to make it last longer.

• When doing needlepoint, cover the rough edges of your canvas with masking tape to keep the yarn from catching and fraying.

• Line up a piece of masking tape on the right side of the 5/8 inch mark (or other desired stitching line) of the sewing machine to make sewing faster and more accurate.

• Place two small pieces of masking tape on the sole of a slippery new shoe to provide just enough traction for the first wear.

• When you take pictures down to move them, attach the hooks to the back with tape to save time when you rehang them.

• Wrap a small piece of masking tape around the center of picture wire to prevent slipping.

• Wrap one end of chalk with masking tape. Your writing hand will stay dust-free, and if you drop the chalk there's less mess.

• Keep a roll of masking tape in the kitchen to date and label anything to be stored in the refrigerator or freezer.

• To remove a lipstick spot from silk, place a piece of masking tape over the stain and quickly yank it off. Dab any remaining color with chalk or talcum powder.

• Cover half the holes in the top of a can of scouring powder with masking tape to better control the amount you shake out.

• If you ruin the adhesive tab on a disposable diaper, simply tape it with masking tape.

• Cover a burned-out headlight with reflector tape until you can get to a service station.

TAPE, REFLECTOR

• Put reflector tape on your dog's or cat's collar to make the animal more visible at night.

- Put strips of bright reflector tape on some old coffee cans and store them in your car trunk to use as safety markers in an emergency.

- If cellar or outdoor stairways are poorly lit, apply reflector tape along the edges of the steps.

TAPE, TRANS-PARENT

- Trim children's bangs by placing a piece of transparent tape across the wet hair and cutting above the tape. You'll have a straight line and fewer loose hairs will fall.

- Put a piece of tape on the wall before driving a nail. If you need to remove the nail, the tape will keep the paint from peeling off.

- Put some tape on a small child's wrist to occupy him or her while you are taking a picture. Or between fingers, to keep a hungry baby in a highchair busy.

- Before the boxes of well-loved games and puzzles begin to fall apart, reinforce the corners with tape.

- If the mouth of a vase is too wide for your bouquet, reduce the size of the opening by placing strips of tape across the top. Crisscross several strips so flowers can be arranged in the various openings.

- When you lose the end of your plastic wrap, touch a piece of tape to it to pick up the edge.

- If a button with a shank is threatening to come off, wrap a thin strip of tape around the last remaining threads until you can fix it. If it's a button with holes, put the tape over the top of it.

- To ease yarn through a tapestry needle, put a bit of transparent tape around the end of the yarn and scissor trim the end to fit the eye.

- When sewing on hooks and eyes or snaps, tape them to the garment so they will be easier to sew and won't slip. When you're through, pull the tape off. Hold a sewing pattern on the material with transparent tape. When cutting the pattern, you will be left with a reinforced edge.

- Tape an address label to your gas cap so that it may be returned if left at the station accidentally.

- When painting, protect the crystal of your watch by covering it with a strip of transparent tape.

- Remove newsprint from fingers by dabbing it off with tape until you get a chance to use soap and water.

- Experiment with different colored nail polish by applying to small pieces of tape over your nails. The tape won't peel off existing polish. Or use transparent tape to make fake fingernails for children (at Halloween time shape into long witch's nails).

- String popcorn at holiday time by dipping a long strip of tape into a bowl of popcorn. You can wrap it on your tree or use it as a garland.

- Stop reflections from lights in the room on digital clocks or VCR's by covering the information area with one or more strips of transparent tape.

TENNIS BALLS

- Tie a tennis ball in an old sock for a dog toy.

- For a quick foot massage, step on a tennis ball on the floor and gently roll your foot around on the ball.

- Hang a tennis ball on a string from the garage ceiling so it will hit the windshield just at the spot where you want your car parked.

- Put 3 or 4 tennis balls in the dryer with your down-filled coat to help fluff the down.

- Catch unreachable cobwebs by wrapping a tennis ball in a dust rag and tossing it into the cobwebbed corner.

- To protect your hand while unscrewing a light bulb from its socket if it's hot or broken, use an old tennis ball cut in half.

- Cut a tennis ball in halves or quarters and tape them to protruding sharp corners that might be dangerous to a small child.

- Clean artificial flowers and plants with an old toothbrush dipped in sudsy water.

- Make a "spatter painting" by using an old toothbrush to "scrub" the paint through a piece of screening onto paper. It's an especially effective technique on paper covered by leaves, weeds, flowers or cut-out stencils.

- Use the handles from old toothbrushes to stake small plants.

- Give a teething infant a clean toothbrush to chew on to ease the pain.

- Use an old toothbrush for grooming eyebrows.

- A clean, old toothbrush is good for manicures and pedicures. It is gentle, yet effective.

- Use a toothbrush to clean combs: just dip it in alcohol and scrub each side of the comb. The method is equally good for typewriter keys.

- Use a toothbrush to clean around the faucets and between the tiles in the bathroom, to clean telephone dials, costume jewelry, the crack on shoes where sole meets leather, around the stove burners and the can opener blade.

- Use an old toothbrush (after you've run it through a dishwasher cycle) to clean a food grater.

- Keep a toothbrush in the laundry room to scrub stains on cloth before washing.

- Use a clean toothbrush as a substitute for a mushroom brush.

- Use a toothbrush to remove lint from the Velcro® on children's sneakers.

- Use a clean toothbrush to spread oil evenly on the surface of a waffle iron. It can also aid in the cleanup: use to brush burned batter from the crevices.

TOOTH-PASTE

- Remove stubborn smells from hands with toothpaste—it even works on fishy smells!

- Use toothpaste to remove spots or stains on polyester clothing, ink spots from cloth, and spots from dress shoes.

- Rub food color stains with toothpaste and allow to dry before washing.

- Use a small dab of white toothpaste as emergency filler for little holes left in the wall from picture nails.

- The next time you drop a glob of toothpaste in the bathroom sink, use it for a quick and easy cleanup. It will even polish the chrome faucet.

- Use toothpaste to scrub crayon marks off painted walls and to clean silver. This is especially handy when silver earrings need polishing while traveling.

- Try toothpaste to remove the yellow stains on your nails that you get from nail polish.

- To remove colored drink "moustaches" from kids' faces, rub on toothpaste and rinse. It tastes pleasant and the kids won't mind.

- To remove tar from the bottom of bare feet, use toothpaste.

- Make a scratch on the crystal of a watch disappear by rubbing toothpaste over it.

- Make "sour" baby bottles smell sweet by scrubbing with toothpaste and a bottle brush.

- Some teenagers have found toothpaste effective on pimples. They dab it on at night before going to bed.

- Hang a poster on a wall using a dab of toothpaste in each corner instead of nails. When the poster eventually comes down, just wipe the wall clean.

TOOTH-PICKS

- When marinating foods that require a whole clove of garlic, skewer it with a toothpick so it's easy to remove when the food is served.

- Insert a toothpick between the lid and the pot to keep just enough steam escaping to prevent boiling over. Try the same trick with a casserole dish in the oven.

- When decorating cake frosting, trace the design or message with a toothpick, then squeeze frosting along the lines.

- To use bottled salad oil sparingly and without measuring, make a shaker top for it by punching 2 or 3 holes in the foil seal with a toothpick.

- Keep small slices of bread from disappearing into your toaster by sticking a toothpick through the top of the bread so that the toothpick lies across the toaster.

- When cooking sweet and spicy sausages at the same time, try putting a toothpick in each of the spicy ones, to identify them.

- To keep frying sausage links from rolling around in the pan, put toothpicks between pairs of them. This helps keep them flat and they need to be turned only once for browning.

- Identify rare, medium rare and medium well steaks or chops on the grill or stovetop with colored toothpicks.

- Use a round toothpick to push fabric, lace or gathers under the pressure foot when sewing.

- Use a toothpick to apply glue to sequins or beads.

- Touch up chipped or scratched paint with a toothpick.

- Dip a toothpick in rubbing alcohol to make short work of cleaning the crevices around the buttons or dial of a telephone.

- When a cupboard door hinge screw becomes loose, insert a toothpick into the hole and re-screw.

- If you lose a screw from eyeglasses, substitute a round wooden toothpick tip until you can get it replaced.

- If you burn yourself lighting candles, try lighting them with wooden toothpicks.

- Stick toothpicks into the bottoms of small birthday candles before putting them on the cake.

- Stick toothpicks to the ends of your rolls of masking or cellophane tape so you don't lose them.

- Give first aid to a broken plant stem by making a splint with a toothpick and tape.

- Use three toothpicks to root an avocado. Make three holes around the avocado seed with a sharp nail and insert toothpicks into each, making sure they are secure. Fill a glass with water and balance the avocado on top, using the toothpicks, with the pointed end of the seed in the water. Place on a window ledge. Soon a root and shoot will appear. When the shoot has leaves, snip off the top to let the avocado tree branch out. Pot it when the roots are thick.

- For a quick dusting job, wrap your arm in an old towel and whisk it across the table and dresser tops.

- When washing good china and crystal, line the sink with a terry-cloth towel to guard against chips and scratches.

TOWELS

- To buff a newly waxed floor and get exercise at the same time, wrap an old bath towel around each foot and "skate" around the floor.

- Clean oven racks by placing them on an old bath towel in the bathtub and soaking them in a solution of ammonia and hot water.

- If you don't have a sleeve board, insert a rolled-up towel in sleeves so they can be pressed without leaving creases.

- To keep the bowl from slipping while mixing ingredients, place it on a folded damp towel on the counter or in the sink.

- Use a dish towel under food plates on a serving tray so dishes don't slide—or at least to absorbs spills, should they occur.

- To keep children from locking themselves in the bathroom, drape a small towel over the top of the door.

- Protect a child against burns from a hot car seat by stretching a light colored towel over the seat to keep the sun off. (The towel also serves as a crumb catcher.)

- Wrap a kitchen shower gift in a striped kitchen towel. Decorate the package with a plastic or copper scouring pad or colorful plastic measuring spoons.

- A colorful beach towel makes a nice bedspread.

- An old bath towel folded and stitched to form a small "pillow-case" makes a perfect cover for a hot water bottle.

TWIST-TIES

- Wrap different colored twist-ties around regularly used electric cords to quickly identify the appliance you want to disconnect.

- Hang Christmas ornaments with twist-ties.

- To keep matching buttons together, string them on a wire twist-tie and twist it closed.

- To keep the plastic bag liner from falling down inside the wastebasket, pull it tight around the top and take up the slack with a twist-tie. When the bag is full, use the twist-tie to close the bag.

VEGETABLE PEELER

- If you need soft butter immediately, use the vegetable peeler.

- Use a vegetable peeler to pare off thin cheese slivers or to make chocolate flakes from a chilled block of chocolate.

- Take the rind off oranges and lemons with a vegetable peeler.

- Use the tip of a vegetable peeler to pit cherries.

- In an emergency, sharpen a pencil with a vegetable peeler.

- Dig out deep-rooted dandelions with an old vegetable peeler.

VELCRO®

- To cut down on pet shedding in the house, staple strips of Velcro® around the pet's flexible door. When the animal brushes against the strips, loose hair will stay behind.

- When the plastic adjustment strap on the back of a baseball-type cap wears out, replace it with strips of Velcro®.

- Put Velcro® on the four corners of indoor and outdoor tablecloths and chair cushions to keep them from shifting or blowing away.

- Can't find the remote control? Use 2 strips of Velcro® to tape it to the side of the TV. Attach the rough-sided strip to the back of the remote control, and it will also adhere to fabric upholstery on a chair or couch.

- To clear lime deposits out of faucets, put 1/3 to 1/2 cup vinegar in a plastic sandwich bag. Tie the bag to the faucet so the entire end is in the vinegar. Leave on for a couple of hours.

- Use a vinegar and water solution to remove soapy film from counter tops.

- Use vinegar to freshen lunch boxes. Dampen a piece of fresh bread with white vinegar and put it in the lunch box overnight.

- To loosen hard to clean stains in glass, aluminum or porcelain pots or pans, boil a solution of white vinegar with water in the pan. Wash in hot, soapy water.

- Boil white vinegar in water to eliminate unpleasant cooking odors in the kitchen.

- Rinse the peanut butter and mayonnaise jars you save with white vinegar to eliminate the odor of the former contents.

- When rinsing dishes in a sink full of hot water, add a capful of vinegar to cut any grease or excess soap. This will give your dishes a clean, sparkling look.

- Drink 1 teaspoon of vinegar in 1/2 cup water to quiet an upset stomach.

- Put a few drops of vinegar in the water to help poached eggs hold their shape.

- To clean the water line from a vase, rub it with a vinegar-soaked paper towel.

- Eliminate odors in smoke-filled rooms during and after a party by placing a small bowl of white vinegar in the room. This also works to remove paint odor.

- Remove old decals by painting them with several coats of white vinegar or covering them with a cloth soaked in vinegar. After several minutes the decals should wash off easily.

- Use vinegar to get animal urine stains out of carpet. Blot up as much of the puddle as possible. Flush with several applications of clean, lukewarm water. Then apply a solution of equal parts of white vinegar and cool water. Blot up excess liquid, rinse with clear water, let the spot dry. If stain remains, apply vinegar solution and allow to remain on the stain for about 15 minutes. Blot up, rinse and let dry.

- To remove wallpaper, mix equal parts vinegar and hot water. Dip a paint roller into the solution, wet the paper thoroughly. After two applications, most paper will peel off in sheets.

- Fill a spray bottle or mister with vinegar to chase away ants.

- Soak dentures overnight in white vinegar to soften tartar enough to easily brush it away with a toothbrush.

- Remove salt stains on shoes and boots by wiping them with a solution of equal parts of white vinegar and warm water. Do it as soon as possible. Polish leather shoes and boots after removing salt.

• Keep swimmer's ear from ruining your child's summer (or your own). One important step is keeping the ear canals dry. Mix equal parts vinegar and rubbing alcohol and put a few drops in each ear canal a few times a day, particularly after swimming, to gently and comfortably dry out the ears.

• Get rid of stains left by deodorants and antiperspirants on washables by lightly rubbing the spots with white vinegar before laundering.

• To keep lint from clinging to corduroys and blue jeans, add 1 cup vinegar to each wash load.

• Clean the hoses and unclog soap scum from your washing machine by pouring a gallon of distilled vinegar into it and running the machine through its entire cycle.

• After washing a wool sweater, rinse it in vinegar water to remove any odor.

• Wash your plastic shower curtain in the washing machine. Add 1 cup vinegar to the rinse cycle. Tumble dry with 1 or 2 towels.

• For beautiful azaleas, add 2 tablespoons of vinegar to a quart of water and use occasionally around these plants which love acidic soil.

• Pour white vinegar on unwanted grasses to get rid of them, especially in crevices and between bricks. It's safe, inexpensive and non-toxic.

WADING POOLS

- Use a filled wading pool as a "stepping stone" to your pool. Have kids dunk their feet in it, leaving dirt and residue there before they jump in. At a beach house, set a pool by the door for kids to wash off sand before entering.

- To protect the sand in the sandbox when no one's playing in it, invert a wading pool over it.

- Pile leaves in the wading pool in the fall and pull them easily to the compost pile.

- Buy a small, inflatable plastic pool to use for bathing on camping trips.

- Since wading pools are so easy to slide under a bed, use them for toy bins, storage of craft items, and out-of-season clothing.

- A small inflatable pool makes an excellent temporary crib for a small baby.

- Make an indoor sandbox by filling a wading pool with birdseed and adding sand toys. Be sure the child is old enough not to eat the birdseed.

- Use a wading pool, lined with newspapers, as a kennel for new puppies or kittens. The mother can reach them, it's waterproof and the sides are high enough to keep them in—for awhile!

- Use fringed terrycloth washcloths for children's napkins.

- Clean a cut or scrape with a red washcloth. The blood won't show and the child won't be frightened.

- Give your child a dry washcloth to hold over his or her forehead during a shampoo. It will absorb the soapy water and keep it from running into eyes.

- Worn-out washcloths make great interfacing for homemade pot holders.

- Dampen a washcloth with liquid fabric softener and toss it in the dryer with your clothes. It's much cheaper than commercial softener sheets.

- Put a folded washcloth in the bottom of your soap dish to absorb water and avoid a messy dish.

WAX PAPER

- Ice cube trays won't stick to the freezer compartment if you put wax paper under the tray.

- Remove fat from soups by laying a piece of wax paper directly on the surface of the liquid, then refrigerate it. When cool, congealed grease will come off with the paper.

- After washing the wooden salad bowl in lukewarm water, dry it thoroughly, then rub it inside and out with wax paper to keep the surface of the bowl sealed.

- When frosting a cake, put strips of wax paper between the cake and the plate. When you're through, pull each piece out gently and the cake plate will be clean and free of crumbs.

- To save cleanup time, keep a sheet of wax paper on the glass heating tray of the microwave. If a spill occurs, throw it out and replace it with a new sheet.

- Roll out biscuits and pastries on a sheet of wax paper with a few drops of water under it to make it adhere to the counter. Easy cleanup!

- When whipping cream, cut the center out of a piece of waxed paper and fit it around the electric mixer beaters to keep the kitchen from getting splattered.

- If you have difficulty removing waffles sticking to the waffle iron, try this: put two sheets of wax paper into the waffle iron and let it heat. When the paper becomes very brown, remove it and add the batter, which now won't stick to the grids.

- Rub wax paper over closet rods to make the hangers slide easily.

- To make lace collars and cuffs look crisp and fresh, iron them between two sheets of wax paper. Lay plain brown paper under and over it to keep melted wax off the ironing board cover and iron.

- To keep an iron skillet from rusting between camping trips, heat it sightly and rub wax paper over it. The coating protects the skillet but doesn't affect food flavor.

- For a quick shine, tie wax paper around your dustmop and rub it over a clean floor.

- After putting white polish on baby shoes, wait until they are dry, then rub with wax paper to get the excess polish off. The white polish will not make marks on parents' dark clothing.

- Crochet hooks and knitting needles sometimes need a good cleanup: wash and dry them, then rub with wax paper.

- A rusty slide will become slick again as your children slide down on big pieces of wax paper.

- To preserve colorful autumn leaves, place them between two sheets of waxed paper (with brown paper over and under them) and press with a warm—not hot—iron.

- You can duplicate the Sunday comics on a piece of wax paper by rubbing firmly with your nail, a popsicle stick or a dull knife.

And one last tip:
    Use the empty, closed box from the wax paper (or any similar container) to hold a hand of cards, for those hands too small or pained to easily hold cards in a game.

Other books by Vicki Lansky:

- FEED ME I'M YOURS cookbook.....$7.95 (spiral).....$4.50 paperback
- TAMING OF THE CANDY MONSTER cookbook.....$7.95
- KIDS COOKING.....$4.95
- MICROWAVE COOKING FOR KIDS.....$4.95
- PRACTICAL PARENTING™ TIPS: YEARS 1-5.....$6.95
- PRACTICAL PARENTING™ TIPS: SCHOOL YEARS.....$5.95
- BEST OF THE PRACTICAL PARENTING™ NEWSLETTER.....$5.95
- TOILET TRAINING.....$3.95
- KOKO BEAR'S NEW POTTY.....$3.95
- WELCOMING YOUR SECOND BABY.....$5.95
- A NEW BABY AT KOKO BEAR'S HOUSE.....$4.95
- DEAR BABYSITTER HANDBOOK.....$3.95
- KOKO BEAR'S NEW BABYSITTER.....$3.95
- KOKO BEAR'S BIG EARACHE (Preparing for Ear Tube Surgery).....$4.95
- GETTING YOUR CHILD TO SLEEP...AND BACK TO SLEEP.....$6.95
- (audio tape with lullabyes) GETTING YOUR BABY TO SLEEP.....$9.95
- BABY PROOFING BASICS.....$5.95
- BIRTHDAY PARTIES: BEST TIPS & IDEAS FOR AGES 1-8.....$6.95
- SING ALONG BIRTHDAY FUN (book & music tape).....$5.95
- SING ALONG AS YOU RIDE ALONG (book & music tape).....$5.95
- 101 WAYS TO TELL YOUR CHILD "I LOVE YOU".....$6.95
- 101 WAYS TO MAKE YOUR CHILD FEEL SPECIAL.....$5.95
- 101 WAYS TO SAY "I LOVE YOU" (for grown-ups).....$6.95
  and, if necessary:
- *Vicki Lansky's* DIVORCE BOOK FOR PARENTS:
  Helping Kids Cope With Divorce and its Aftermath.....$4.50

To order these books or additional copies of ANOTHER USE FOR...101
Common Household Items ($6.95) by phone (MC/Visa) call:
PRACTICAL PARENTING at 1-800-255-3379.
Or for a free catalog of all these titles write to:
Practical Parenting, Dept AUF, Deephaven, MN 55391.